Conducting
Needs
Assessments

SAGE HUMAN SERVICES GUIDES

A series of books edited by ARMAND LAUFFER and CHARLES D. GARVIN. Published in cooperation with the University of Michigan School of Social Work and other organizations.

Conducting
Needs
Assessments

A Multidisciplinary
Approach

Fernando I. Soriano

SHSG SAGE HUMAN SERVICES GUIDE 68

*Published in cooperation with the University
of Michigan School of Social Work*

SAGE Publications
International Educational and Professional Publisher
Thousand Oaks   London   New Delhi

96-592

For information address:

SAGE Publications, Inc.
2455 Teller Road
Thousand Oaks, California 91320

SAGE Publications Ltd.
6 Bonhill Street
London EC2A 4PU
United Kingdom

SAGE Publications India Pvt. Ltd.
M-32 Market
Greater Kailash I
New Delhi 110 048 India

Printed in the United States of America

Library of Congress Cataloging-in-Publication Data

Soriano, Fernando I.
    Conducting needs assessments: A multidisciplinary approach/
Fernando I., Soriano.
      p. cm. —(Sage human services guides; 68)
    Includes bibliographical references
    ISBN 0-8039-5211-2 (cloth: acid-free paper). — ISBN 0-8039-5212-0
(pbk.: acid-free paper).
    1. Human services—United States—Evaluation. 2. Social service—
United States—Evaluation. 3. Needs assessment—United States.
I. Title. II. Series: Sage human services guides; v. 68.
HV91.S6267   1995
362.3'2'068—dc20   95-10015

This book is printed on acid-free paper.

95 96 97 98 99   10 9 8 7 6 5 4 3 2 1

Production Editor: Astrid Virding   Typesetter: Christina M. Hill

This book is dedicated to my sons Fernando and Anthony—
the most important and precious experiences in my life thus far.

CONTENTS

PREFACE

During my tenure as research psychologist for the Navy Personnel Research and Development Center in San Diego in the early 1980s I first became interested and involved in conducting needs assessments. With the establishment of Navy Family Service Centers throughout Navy bases worldwide, concomitant with looming military budget cuts, base commanders were being asked to undertake needs assessments of military personnel and their dependents. At that time the military and Navy were dramatically expanding their interest in military families, because studies were suggesting a link between their well-being and such military concerns as performance, readiness, and retention. Similarly, my subsequent work with community-based agencies involved me with needs assessments. Altogether, these experiences demonstrated to me the importance of needs assessments and pointed to the lack of information available about this powerful assessment concept and tool.

My interaction with those needing and benefiting from needs assessments has prompted me to write this book. It is written to be easy to read, yet technically sophisticated and comprehensive enough to address such critical questions as knowing the first steps to plan for an assessment, determining sample sizes, conducting appropriate analyses, and the best formats for reporting findings. An important feature of this book is Chapter 8, on special considerations in working with culturally and socially diverse populations. From the start, the United States has been multicultural and socially diverse, which is the case now more than ever. Conducting successful needs assessments necessitates taking into consideration the inherent diversity of target populations—whether based on culture, gender, income, education, or regional differences. It is my hope that readers will find this book as helpful, practical, and approachable as it was intended to be.

Many people helped with this book. First and foremost, Sandy and my boys afforded me not only the time I spent writing the book, but also the time I spent earlier conducting needs assessments or helping others to do so. Second, I acknowledge the many military and civilian community leaders who helped me better understand what type of information is lacking on needs assessments. In particular, I wish to thank Ann O'Keefe who, as head of the Navy's Family Support Program at the time, made it possible for me to continue my involvement in needs assessments. The support, encouragement, and trust granted to me by Dean Michael Reed and my Department Chair Philip Feil of the University of Missouri were essential to the completion of this book. I wish also to acknowledge the support of my mother, Ignacia Soriano, who was always there to validate my efforts, no matter what they were. I wish to acknowledge the recent and significant contributions of Elena Marie Melendez, who was interested enough in needs assessments to donate her deft editorial skills.

Last but certainly not least, I wish to express my deep appreciation to series editor Armand Lauffer and Marquita Flemming from Sage—who both were abundantly patient and encouraging in the journey of writing this book. Without their patience and understanding I would never have completed it. More recently, James Nageotte, also from Sage, became the book's editor and accomplished many detailed editorial and publication tasks. To him I also owe great gratitude for his skillful editorial assistance. This book, minus its shortcomings, is a tribute to Lauffer, Flemming, and Nageotte.

—FERNANDO I. SORIANO

INTRODUCTION

David, I really don't know. We have been funding your community center for the past five years and have always trusted your judgment in offering needed services. I've kept up with the newspaper articles reporting the many events you have sponsored in the community. The annual reports you provided have been appreciated. You've always listed the activities in which your center has participated. But, David, we are swamped with requests from others in the city who are looking for support and need our help. And frankly, they do have empirical data clearly demonstrating the need for their proposed programs. I'm sorry, David, but without data showing the need for your services, we can no longer fund your center.

Human service providers are increasingly confronted with the need to prove that their services are indeed needed. Although in the past this proof could have been verification that services were being rendered, now service providers are likely to be required to demonstrate a clear awareness of their target population. The above vignette illustrates the increasing demand for empirical data to justify funding for human service programs. As a result, many representatives of the social and human service fields will be involved in commissioning, conducting, or utilizing information from needs assessments—if not for justifying services, then for determining what they should be.

The term *needs assessment* appears deceptively simple to understand. It refers to the process of assessing needs. Some might say that it means the collection of data bearing on the need for services, products, or information. In fact, it is the conceptually appealing nature of the term that makes its frequent application attractive. Unfortunately, although the term seems intuitive, the process of conducting needs assessments is far from intuitive. Rather, it is technical and sophisticated. And it requires an awareness of the scope and significance of the information collected.

Kaufman and English (1979) describe needs assessment in a way that reflects this complexity. They call it "a tool for determining valid and useful problems which are philosophically as well as practically sound. It keeps us from running down more blind educational alleys, from using time, dollars and people in attempted solutions which do not work" (p. 31). From this definition, we can conclude that needs assessments enable us to obtain valid and reliable information, which helps us to better target our services and efforts. Private businesses readily recognize the importance of evaluating the need for their products or services. A lack of need for what they offer translates into no sales. Their immediate criteria for success are sales and profits. On the other hand, in the human services realm, in particular among not-for-profit organizations, the volume of sales and profits is not the driving force. Typically, their criterion for success is providing the services they recognize are needed in their catchment area. The need for social programs or human services is too often only assumed or believed evident and efforts to measure it are lacking. Among those who attempt to conduct needs assessments, many fail to know how to do so, which commonly results in uninterpretable or unrepresentative information gathered.

The demand for a better understanding of needs assessments is changing, however. This phenomenon is largely due to the diminishing of monies available for human service providers. The requirement for the empirical demonstration of the need for services will undoubtedly continue in the years to come. The lack of available resources has led to increased competition for funding among services. Unfortunately, subjective appeals from service providers for funding for their services will no longer be sufficient. To ensure that limited monies are appropriated for the most useful services, funders are demanding clearer justification for programming budgets.

Many funding agencies and foundations are requiring that applications for funding include results from needs assessments that demonstrate a clear need for the proposed programs or services. This requirement has led to a significant increase in the number of needs assessments being conducted for and by agencies. However, as those who are engaged in assessments are finding, the term needs assessment is often easier to comprehend than to apply. Moreover, serious measurement risks can result from conducting improper needs assessments. A needs assessment conducted in the general community, for example, may reveal a need for drug abuse treatment services, but may not be specific enough to point out the particular service needs of certain subpopulations such as the homeless, the highly transient, ethnic minority groups, non-English speakers, and so on. Needs assessments can be misleading when not carefully planned and executed.

There are myriad reasons for conducting needs assessments, whether from requirements imposed by entities external to an organization or those requested internally. The following are among the most common reasons:

- Justification for funding
- Regulations or laws that mandate needs assessments
- Resource allocation and decision making—determining the best use of limited resources
- Assessing the needs of specific, underserved subpopulations
- As part of program evaluations

As mentioned earlier, funding agencies are increasingly demanding empirical justification for the financial support they provide. Furthermore, a growing number of state and federal agencies, as well as private foundations, mandate that funded agencies and programs conduct periodic needs assessments to ensure that funds are being used for services that are most needed.

The mandate for program justification is not the only driving force behind the implementation of need assessments. Interest in such studies comes from various sources and situations. Successful, established service programs often recognize that needs assessments can help them to prioritize their efforts for the greatest possible programmatic effect. Results from needs assessments are used to make decisions about internal programming and resource allocation. In contrast, tragic social upheavals, such as the Los Angeles riots, also cause agencies and programs to reevaluate their effectiveness in meeting the needs of underserved communities. Well-targeted needs assessments can do much to identify the needs of frequently overlooked subpopulations, including ethnic minorities, adolescents, women, single parents, the elderly, and the homeless.

Given the right planning, needs assessments can also form part of a program evaluation effort. Used in this way, needs assessments are conducted both before and after programmatic efforts are in place. The directors of a drug abuse prevention program may, for example, decide that the effectiveness of their community awareness campaigns can be reflected in both the reduction of use and in the perceived need for drug abuse prevention services. Hence, they may decide that changes suggested by responses to pre- and postneeds assessments will form part of their program evaluation. They can also use the results from each assessment to prioritize their services.

Agencies and programs commonly have multiple reasons for conducting or commissioning needs assessments—some externally imposed, others internally derived. In many cases, needs assessments that are implemented at the request of an external agency would not otherwise be initiated. The perceived imposition of having to conduct an assessment leads to the term engendering strongly negative connotations since it is viewed as a threat or a burden. Consequently programs required to conduct needs assessments by outside agencies are often the least motivated to utilize the information gained from the reports for their own purposes. In contrast, agencies and programs that recognize the value of empirical information are the most likely to benefit from these assessments.

Whether initiated internally or externally, whether viewed as a hassle or a help, needs assessments can help ensure programmatic success and efficiency by providing timely information about the communities being served. Human service programs and organizations are, by virtue of their mission, dynamic and evolving. Their effectiveness and survival increasingly depend on the availability of objective data guiding their efforts. This book is designed to help agencies, programs, researchers, and others better understand needs assessment methodologies.

This book is suitable for use in courses, workshops, and as part of the reference material of human service agencies and organizations. It is designed to provide a basic but working understanding of needs assessments. I will focus on the methods commonly used in conducting needs assessments for application in human or social services. This book is structured as a practical, "how-to" resource, guiding the reader through the steps required to undertake a comprehensive needs assessment. It begins with the formulation of realistic objectives and ends with a discussion of effective reporting formats. Each chapter contains examples, suggestions, and exercises for developing basic research competencies. A needs assessment guide is included in the appendix, which guides the user through each conceptual and empirical step outlined in the book.

This book is meant not as a substitute for but as a complement to an earlier volume on needs assessments in this series by Sage (Neuber et al., 1980). Unlike the earlier volume, which presented one needs assessment methodology and model, this book examines the most commonly used methodologies for conducting needs assessments. The reader is encouraged to consult other volumes in this series for other relevant and useful information also bearing on needs assessments (Berger & Patchner, 1988a, 1988b; Blythe & Tripodi, 1989; Coley & Scheinberg, 1990; Kettner, Moroney, & Martin, 1990; Lauffer, 1982; Schaefer, 1987).

A special feature of this book is its multidisciplinary approach to needs assessments. Other publications have typically been grounded in a particular discipline, such as business or mental health. Another advantage of this book is that it assumes a candid and pragmatic approach to conducting needs assessments. Too often, those commissioned to conduct needs assessments fail to understand the organizational limitations to utilizing new information; thus, their suggestions assume organizational change is both easy and welcome. New information may not be accepted by the agency, for reasons that vary from political motivations (maintenance of the status quo) to pragmatic reasons such as budgetary constraints.

OVERVIEW

The presentation of topics in the book's chapters follows a conceptual and practical sequence that plots out the steps for conducting needs assessments. Chapter 1 describes and distinguishes needs assessments from other related efforts, such as program evaluation. Included is a discussion of the limitations facing agencies and programs undertaking needs assessments. Several common needs assessment methodologies are introduced and described in Chapter 2. Chapter 3 considers in greater depth survey methods, which are most common and popular, and includes a simplified discussion of what is often a misunderstood issue: sample size and selection. Connected to sample size requirements are participation and nonresponse rates, also discussed in Chapter 3. Guidelines for developing data collection instruments are discussed in Chapter 4.

Statistical methods are introduced and their applications described in Chapter 5. Chapter 6 discusses traditional and effective methods of reporting findings. Throughout the book a concerted effort is made to mention special considerations when working with socially, linguistically, and culturally diverse populations. However, special theoretical, conceptual, and methodological considerations are outlined in Chapter 7, to assist those conducting needs assessments with diverse populations. Finally, the Conclusion points to additional resource materials that the reader may investigate, including a description of the Needs Assessment Resource Guide, which is included in this book.

Chapter 1

PLANNING A NEEDS ASSESSMENT

A community-based organization decides to conduct a needs assessment because those funding the agency require it before their grant is renewed. Michael Smith, a program coordinator, is chosen to perform the study, but is assigned the task only as a collateral duty. Michael has never undertaken needs assessments and knows very little about conducting a study. "Well, Michael," asks the agency's executive director, "how are your plans coming along for the needs assessment?"

Using the preceding example, what would the coordinator's first steps be to accomplish the assigned task? Can the coordinator accomplish the task by himself? This chapter discusses various up-front decisions to be made as well as the background information to be collected before undertaking a needs assessment. Preliminary steps include:

- Distinguishing needs assessments from program evaluations
- Understanding the purpose of an assessment
- Acknowledging the limitations of assessments
- Deciding on the necessary level of complexity
- Knowing the resource limitations
- Knowing how the study's findings will be applied

PROGRAM EVALUATION
VERSUS NEEDS ASSESSMENTS

Needs assessments are frequently confused with program evaluation efforts. To some people, having to collect information that would alter an existing agency's services smacks of program evaluation. A needs assessment may indeed be considered a form of evaluation, because it may

1

suggest that some of the current services are not needed or are lacking. However, it is important to distinguish between needs assessments and program evaluation efforts, as they have very different purposes. Needs assessments are used to collect data on the need for or current use of services, products, or information. The information gained from needs assessments is typically used to make decisions about the allocation of program resources and services. Program evaluations are more specifically concerned with evaluating the effectiveness or impact of an agency, organization, or program. Program evaluations may well suggest unmet needs, but this is not their primary purpose.

As mentioned in the Introduction, needs assessments can form part of an evaluation, but only when both components are specifically addressed in the effort's objectives and reflected in the data collection instruments. For example, representatives of a five-year delinquency reduction program may decide to conduct two needs assessments—one at the beginning and another at the end of the program's five-year funding term. If the primary objective of the program is to reduce adolescent delinquency by 50% in that community, the measurement of delinquency in the community should be made at the beginning and the end of the five-year program. Prevalence or incidence data regarding delinquency would form the main part of the program evaluation component, while questions on the current use of and need for services could fulfill both evaluation and needs assessment functions.

Even in this example, program evaluations and needs assessments are viewed and treated differently. The information derived from each is intended for different purposes. The program evaluation component would assess the program's current effectiveness, while the needs assessment component would evaluate the use and need for services. Readers interested in learning more about program evaluations are referred to Pietrzak et al. (1990) and Cook and Levitan (1985).

LIMITATIONS OF NEEDS ASSESSMENTS

Before continuing, one caveat about needs assessments is in order. Though much useful and practical information is derived from needs assessments, no assessment is able to quantify perfectly the specific service requirements for any agency or program. Reasons for this include one or a combination of the following:

- A reluctance by needs assessment participants to truly admit the current use of services or to reveal personal concerns about the need for services

- Opposition to disclosing to agencies a need for services, regardless of recognized need for them
- Lack of access to respondents
- Unwillingness by some people to participate in any survey or study
- Purposely deceptive responses given by some
- Poorly written or confusing questions
- Erroneous interpretation of responses

Consequently, rather than being conclusive, needs assessments suggest the *probable* need for services or programs. Collecting information from people is difficult in itself. The wording of a question, for example, is critical to collecting valid and reliable information. Consider the following statement to which a respondent is instructed to indicate level of agreement: "Substance abuse services are definitely needed."

Without further instructions, respondents can easily interpret this question as inquiring about the perception of needs in society in general—outside of the respondents' immediate environment or families. Yet the researcher, in interpreting this question, may mistakenly infer that the responses reflect the perceived need for services in the community or immediate environment. Clearly, questions asked in a needs assessment should have the same meaning for both the respondents and the investigators if the results are intended to be valid and reliable.

Misunderstandings and problems with clarity can be reduced by certain procedures, such as pretesting instruments. Although pretest procedures differ, they typically consist of having about 10 to 20 respondents, who meet the sample selection criteria, review, complete and critique a draft of the assessment instrument. A questionnaire or paper and pencil test is often referred to as an "instrument." The key to effective pretesting is the establishment of rapport with respondents, allowing them to review and critique the procedures and instructions as well as the wording of the questions. Even when developing a self-administering questionnaire (that is, one where subjects do not require assistance), many researchers find it useful to read each question to the respondents during pretesting. After also allowing the respondent to read and respond to each question, the following questions are commonly asked:

- What does this question seem to be asking of you?
- How clear is the question? If it is not clear, what would be a better way of asking it?
- Are the response choices for the question clear and helpful?

After all questions have been read to participants, they are asked about the questionnaire in general and the entire procedure. Examples of such questions:

- Were there questions in the questionnaire that you feel should be left out? If so, why? (e.g., they are redundant?)
- Are there questions not in the questionnaire that should be included, given the purpose of this study?
- Is there anything else about this study that you would like to comment on or have questions about?

Needs assessment instruments are altered according to the feedback given by the pretest subjects. Significant alterations or rewording of questions in the instruments may warrant pretesting them again.

The pretest sample should always mirror the heterogeneity of the target population. For example, a community health center conducting a needs assessment in an area that has 30% African Americans, 30% Latinos, and 40% White non-Latinos should include respondents who reflect the diversity of those demographics. Furthermore, the heterogeneity found in any particular cultural group should likewise be reflected in the pretest sample (e.g., monolingual Spanish-speaking versus monolingual English-speaking Latinos, low-income populations versus middle-income populations, elderly, children).

Conducting an appropriate pretest before fielding (administering) an instrument will greatly improve the validity of the responses. Even so, as mentioned earlier, research that involves people is always imperfect. The reliability and validity of the findings are influenced by such factors as the wording of the questions, the type and number of respondents, the type of statistical analyses used, and the subjective interpretations of the results. The decisions pertaining to these factors obviously bear on the level of validity and complexity of a needs assessment.

SIMPLICITY AND COMPLEXITY

Needs assessments range from very simple studies involving small groups (such as focus groups) to very large and costly surveys involving hundreds of participants. For example, an African American community center in a large midwestern city decides to conduct a needs assessment to better understand the interests of the community residents, so as to increase their use of its facilities and programs. The center may decide to use two needs assessment methods. First, it would use the key informant methodology, gathering a group of other social service agency representatives to obtain their views about how to increase participation. If this method proves inadequate, the center's staff may decide that only the community's residents hold the answers. Thus staff would conduct a community-wide resident study using the survey method.

The preceding example illustrates how needs assessment methods differ in their level of complexity. However, the complexity of a particular methodology does not necessarily reflect its validity or usefulness. A small-scale study, such as a focus group of only a few respondents, can be as valid for certain purposes as a largescale survey. The cross between the specific type of information needed and the most accessible and appropriate method of obtaining that information increases the validity and aptness of the data. For example, the most valid and appropriate method to assess the needs and concerns of Latino youth gang members in Kansas City would not entail a survey method involving large numbers. Rather, a simpler method such as the interview method would provide more accurate and useful information due to the relatively small numbers of gang members.

Subsequent chapters will discuss a range of methods that differ in complexity. Each of these methods has advantages and disadvantages. However, before discussing them, there are other critical issues about needs assessments that need to be considered, including:

- Understanding the *purpose* or reason for the assessment
- Considering the *resources* available to undertake the effort, including funds and people
- Knowing the planned *application* of the study's findings

THE PURPOSE OF A NEEDS ASSESSMENT

Being clear on the purpose of a needs assessment is the first step in the process. As in the earlier scenario of the community worker who is delegated the task of conducting a needs assessment, it is common to delegate responsibility for conducting one without providing guidance to those assigned the task. Understanding the purpose of a needs assessment involves not only understanding the reason(s) for the assessment, but also knowing for whom it is being conducted, why it is being conducted, what information is required, and how much importance will be attached to the results.

Community-based agencies are commonly required to conduct needs assessments as a prerequisite for receiving funding. Many agencies and programs consider such mandates bothersome and waste of time. Many believe they already know the concerns and needs of those they serve. Then again, there are agencies and programs facing the same mandate who would view it as an opportunity to help them prioritize their services. These contrasting reactions show how important it is for the team working on a needs assessment to know how the study is viewed by their agency as well as by those mandating it. Without this understanding, it is easy either to overestimate or deemphasize the importance of the study, which can quickly result in misunderstandings and frustration. Direct, clear, and frequent communication with those calling for a needs assessment is imperative at the onset of any effort.

Those asked to undertake a needs assessment will help give direction to the effort by identifying the *key players* or *stakeholders* with a vested interest in the accomplishment of the task and what they hope will come from it. Stakeholders typically include service agency administrators and funders. However, stakeholders can also include community leaders or others outside the agency who may be critical of the services being rendered and who can bear pressure on it to change. For our purposes, stakeholders are those whose opinion should be considered in forming the purpose, scope, and design of the needs assessment. They include those who will receive, use, and benefit from the results.

After identifying the stakeholders, it is important to delineate what each of the major stakeholders would like to see come out of an assessment and why and how important it is to act on these expectations. To illustrate, imagine a funding representative *(who),* such as a project officer overseeing an AIDS prevention grant who wants a needs assessment conducted on knowledge of risk behavior linked to AIDS that includes sufficient representation of minorities *(what),* because she suspects that differences exist between ethnic groups *(why).* The needs assessment is not being mandated by the project officer for this sole reason, as it is a requirement of all programs awarded such a grant. Talking to the project officer about her expectations for the study reveals that her decision to support continued funding hinges on the agency's deriving specific information that would help develop targeted efforts aimed at cultural groups most in need of information about AIDS prevention *(how important).*

As the preceding example shows, the information derived from a particularly important stakeholder can be used to make such decisions as the type of information to assess and the ethnic representation of the sample. Figure 1.1 illustrates the sequence of four steps needed to develop the

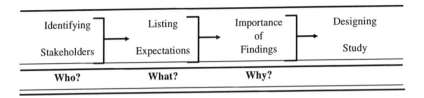

Figure 1.1. Preliminary Sequential Steps Used to Design a Needs Assessment

purpose and design of a needs assessment. Listing the expectations refers to the type of information expected from a needs assessment.

This model for collecting preliminary information does not negate the importance of using one's professional judgment and understanding. The opinions and expectations of stakeholders may not be enough to decide the scope or the subjects covered in a needs assessment. The professional judgment of those conducting the assessment as well as that of others in the service agency or program in question should also be considered. Once the scope of a study is determined, an outline of the subject areas to be covered by the data gathering instrument (e.g., questionnaire) needs to be developed. This step simplifies the development of the items on the questionnaire.

KEY QUESTIONS

Following the inquiry model of who, what, and why, a listing of key questions can be derived to guide in the selection of the best methodology and the development of subject categories for which questions will be derived to address the key questions. For example, a relatively new mental health center in a suburban area was mandated by the city (*who*—the city provides more than half of the center's funding) to conduct a needs assessment among adolescent youth in the city. Over the previous month five high school students were stabbed during fights in school (*why*). There was a concern that youth were becoming more violent because of unknown needs remaining unmet. The new mental health center was seen as the appropriate source to obtain information and treatment for youth. The Parent Teacher Association held an emergency meeting with the mayor complaining that this problem had been ignored for too long. They were prepared to go public with their criticism of the mayor for not addressing violence among youth. The mayor was up for reelection in seven months and feared the issue would be used by her opponents. Therefore, she expected *knowledge* about why the violence and *action* in the form of increased services rendered before the election.

In this scenario, the key stakeholder is the mayor *(who)*. Her reason for prompting a needs assessment was not an overall concern for youth in the city, which would have suggested a broad needs assessment of youth, *(what);* rather the problem was political—dictating a narrower and more targeted response *(why)*. Consequently, the mental health center decided to hold a series of focus groups of students who were directly or indirectly involved in fights at school over the previous year. Focus groups would also be held with parents and school officials.

Two key questions were identified that would guide the type of information sought from the needs assessment:

1. Why was there youth violence in the schools?
2. What could the mental health center do to help?

Some may say, "Of course, these are obvious questions. There's no need to list them." The problem is that those responsible for undertaking a needs assessment commonly get carried away with seeking information that may be relevant but is not necessary. To illustrate this and using the previous example, consider the following list of possible correlates of youth violence that can be conceivably made part of a needs assessment on this topic:

- Domestic violence
- Youth experiences with abuse
- Family functioning
- Substance abuse
- Mental illness
- Experiences with bullies
- Exposure to gangs
- Exposure to violence in the media
- Youth self-esteem
- Academic self-efficacy
- Family economic strain
- Parental employment
- Parental self-esteem
- Parental education
- Youth conflict resolution skills
- Youth communication skills

- Youth future goals and life plans
- Youth culture conflict
- Youth alienation in the schools
- Youth access to weapons

While those generating such a list could be commended for their intuitive sense of the correlates of violence, this list would cause many undertaking a needs assessment to become overwhelmed with measuring all these individual and community characteristics. That is why it is so important to have a clear understanding of the basic information requirements and a small set of key questions that guides and limits the scope of the study.

RESOURCE AVAILABILITY

Interest in and commitment to conducting a needs assessment may be high, but resources to undertake one are often lacking. Limited resources determine the scope and the type of a needs assessment required. Resources involve funds, people, time, and supplies. Ideally, human service organizations would have the funds to contract independent and experienced researchers to conduct their needs assessment. This option is preferable because experienced researchers have the knowledge to effectively guide agency members in outlining and articulating their informational needs. Moreover, they are prepared to help the agency understand the results and their implications.

Realistically, many service agencies do not have the financial resources to pay for researchers to help them conduct needs assessments, so they often must make do with their own personnel and resources. Given the availability and commitment to time, resources, and effort, there are advantages to an agency's conducting its own needs assessment, including having a more intimate understanding of the agency, knowing better the stakeholders and informational needs, and having better access to respondents.

Consider the community worker assigned to undertake a needs assessment as a collateral duty. To conduct a successful needs assessment, he or she needs to consider the availability of resources compared with the expectations and scope of the needs assessment. Unrealistic expectations need to be discussed immediately with supervisors and agency administrators. It is always important to break up the entire effort into steps that can be written on a timeline. Doing so often points out the inadequacy of resources allocated to accomplish the task.

APPLICATION OF FINDINGS

The application of a needs assessment refers to what the agency is prepared to do with the information once it is derived. As mentioned earlier, some service agencies or organizations see needs assessments as imposed requirements—another thing to get done. In these cases usually no plans are made to utilize the information gained. On the other hand, some organizations may be excited about conducting a needs assessment. They may see the generation of information as an end in itself or an intellectual exercise of sorts. Again, no plans are made to utilize the information gained for organizational change. Still others, while wanting to act upon new information, lack the political or organizational support to make necessary changes.

Those who most effectively utilize needs assessment data for organizational improvement are typically successful organizations or agencies that are dynamic and fluid—open to ideas, improvement, and change based upon valid, reliable and logical information. To these dynamic organizations, need assessments are not threats, but opportunities to test current assumptions about the need for services, information, or products. In any case, organizations or agencies undertaking needs assessments need to think about the changes they are willing and able to make based on the information obtained before they gather new information.

EXERCISES

EXAMPLES OF NEEDS ASSESSMENTS

Confusion often exits about the difference between needs assessments and program evaluations. While they may share methodologies, they differ significantly in objectives. The following are examples of each.

Example 1

Job morale and work performance have declined steadily in the membership recruitment division of a large not-for-profit organization. Division managers suspect a need for improving supervisor-employee relations and for better training in the use of computer equipment and desktop publishing software. To address the needs of the division, management has commissioned a one-time needs assessment that focuses on training needs and employee-supervisor relations. There are no plans to evaluate changes of the same needs over time. This, then, cannot concurrently be a needs assessment and an evaluation project. Management has a genuine desire to understand the training problems and is committed to instituting changes based on the study findings. Hence, there is a good possibility that the information derived from the needs assessment will not be simply an intellectual exercise, but an effort leading to significant improvements in the division.

Example 2

The government's recognition of increased youth violence has resulted in new federal monies becoming available for cities to use in addressing this problem. Cities must demonstrate a clear need, along with a plan to address this need, to obtain these funds. A midwestern city decides to conduct a citywide needs assessment, which will be triphased. The methodology chosen includes collecting information from: (a) law enforcement and school representatives—to document problems with youth violence in communities and in the schools, (b) a representative sample of city residents—to assess the public's concern and experience with youth violence, and (c) existing service providers—to indicate needs for more and improved services.

Information from the needs assessment will be used to justify the improvement and increase of existing services. The data will highlight the problems of youth violence and point to specific services needed to address these problems. This is a one-time assessment, with no immediate plans to repeat it. County government officials are working closely with city officials and are prepared to propose changes in services based on the findings. Hence, there is a good probability that the needs assessment will result in an improved understanding of youth violence and of service needs in the city.

EXAMPLES OF PROGRAM EVALUATIONS

Example 1

A coalition of agencies received a five-year community grant from a federal agency concerned with funding programs to reduce illegal drug use. The coalition was composed of law enforcement, school, and city health programs. The coalition focused on reducing illegal drug use among adolescents through school-based presentations that attempted to "scare" teenagers away from using drugs. Law enforcement officials used graphic depictions of victims of violence linked to drug use and sales. They also brought in prisoners to warn youth of the consequences of being caught using drugs. Two comparable schools were chosen to participate in the evaluation. One school participated in the coalition's program, while the other participated in the "Just Say No" program, which focused more on informing about the dangers of drug use. Over the five years, the number of adolescents from each school who were charged with drug use, referred to drug treatment programs, or sent to a counselor for possible drug use was recorded and served as the primary evaluation criteria.

This effort clearly focuses on evaluation. The information is being collected simply to evaluate the effect of the experimental program conducted by the coalition. None of the information collected can serve to assess the service needs of adolescent youth in the schools, though there may well be unmet service needs.

Example 2

A community residential home has been housing the same 15 patients for two years as part of a three-year demonstration project. The residents are chronically depressed patients and were previously hospitalized for catatonic depression. The program was designed to increase patient independence and self-sufficiency by providing individual and group therapy from licensed clinical social workers. Empirical data on the program's impact was needed to obtain continued funding for the project. The evaluation study team assessed the patients': (a) depression scores, (b) sense of independence, (c) employment status and earnings, and (d) sense of preparedness to move out of the home and set up their own residences.

This study is clearly an evaluation and not a needs assessment, since the information gained is not intended to point out the need for new, altered, or improved services. That is, there are no plans to change services based on the study's findings. The impact of the program is the primary concern.

EXAMPLES OF PROJECTS THAT ARE BOTH NEEDS ASSESSMENTS AND PROGRAM EVALUATIONS

Example 1

A school cafeteria had been receiving a growing number of complaints from students and parents about the poor service, low food quality, and high cost of student meals. The number of students buying their lunch at school had steadily decreased in the past six months. A needs assessment was conducted to assess the following attitudes of students and parents: (a) specific complaints about the staff serving the food, (b) dissatisfaction with food, (c) and dissatisfaction with cost. The assessment was done through a questionnaire administered to students and parents. The intent was to first assess their specific concerns within these subject domains.

Then, based on the results of the initial assessment, tailored staff-student relations training and altered menus and prices were provided. Plans were made to administer the same assessment questionnaire every six months.

In this example, the questionnaire initially served to assess the concerns and needs of students and parents (needs assessment). The initial results were then used as a baseline measure, to which results from future surveys would be compared in assessing progress (evaluation).

Example 2

A community uproar occurred over police brutality following an altercation between two intoxicated community members who were arguing with two police officers. An ensuing riot accentuated the poor rapport the police had with the community. To improve its image, the police department was prepared to make any changes recommended by the findings from a community needs assessment. From its inception, the needs assessment was designed to act as both an assessment and an evaluation tool. The community's perceptions of police activity were the main concern of the study and were evaluated through individuals' impressions of: (a) officers' concern for the public's welfare, (b) responsiveness to calls for assistance, (c) courtesy exhibited by officers, both in person and over the phone, (d) appropriateness of actions when involved with the intervention of disorderly conduct or criminal behavior, and (e) observations of inappropriate or undue force used by police.

The plans were to assess the need for better community relations by developing measures in each of the five outlined areas. Then, based on the results of this initial assessment, the goal was to develop internal department training initiatives and programs for community outreach. After one year of instituting changes and programs, another assessment would be made to assess the same needs and concerns of the community and thus to evaluate the impact of the programs implemented.

Suggested Exercises

For each of the preceding examples involving needs assessments:

1. Indicate whether the needs assessment is complex or simple and point out the characteristics that make it so. Consider the advantages and disadvantages of changing the level of simplicity to its opposite (e.g., time, people involved, resources expended).
2. Identify who is requiring the needs assessment, why one is believed necessary, and how much importance the findings have, as well as the extent to which they will be used.

3. Point out possible limitations of the different types of needs assessments (e.g., the validity and reliability of self-perceived judgments by respondents).

Chapter 2

ASSESSMENT METHODS

"Juana!" Paul gushed. "We just got word that the funding for the new teen-age pregnancy prevention program has been approved for the full three years! Now you can start the needs assessment you said you would conduct on the sexual knowledge, attitudes, beliefs, and practices of male and fe-male adolescents in our Latino community. It will be great to use the find-ings to develop awareness and educational campaigns we said we would implement in local middle and high schools. Dr. Jones, our federal project officer, will come to meet with you next week and he wants us to tell him the kind of needs assessment we will be conducting."

As Juana Serros listened to the news, a frown darkened her face.

"But, Paul," she asked, "What kind of a needs assessment is appro-priate?"

Good initial planning will help develop the purpose and outline of the topics to be covered by a needs assessment. However, choosing the most appropriate method is a difficult decision. What makes it so complicated is that different methods can lead to similar, if not identical, conclu-sions. However, various factors can help in choosing the best methods. This chapter will review some of these factors, then describe five commonly used needs assessment methods: (a) secondary data, (b) in-terview, (c) key informant, (d) small group, and (e) forecasting. Because of their popularity, survey methods will be discussed separately in the following chapter.

DECIDING WHICH NEEDS
ASSESSMENT METHOD TO USE

Three main factors help us decide which method is best:

1. Time
2. Resources (funding and personnel)
3. Knowledge

Each needs assessment method differs in the time needed for implementation, the number of people involved, the funding resources required, and the technical knowledge needed. No method is perfect or inherently better than others. How methods differ—their strengths and weaknesses and the level of time, resources, and knowledge required to implement them—will be discussed in this chapter. First, I will consider the use of secondary data sources, one of the simplest and most cost-effective methods.

USE OF SECONDARY DATA SOURCES

What better way to meet information needs than to use existing data. Utilizing existing data represents the secondary data method of conducting needs assessments. Cities, counties, states, and national organizations routinely collect and maintain many types of data. They undertake periodic surveys on a host of topics such as health, crime, victimization, employment, and education. A wealth of demographic characteristics on diverse populations is conveniently maintained by these organizations. For example, those interested in assessing the mental health status of residents in a particular community can often find useful and sufficient data by simply contacting city or state departments of health or mental health.

Even if the collection of new data is warranted, using secondary data can enhance newly collected data. Moreover, many of the offices that maintain secondary data typically have resident researchers and/or statisticians who can help guide individuals and groups in designing and conducting needs assessments as well as assisting with data analysis. Two examples demonstrate the use of secondary data in lieu of a needs assessment. In the first example, demographic data are strictly used to assess the need for substance abuse services. In the second example, secondary data are used to augment newly collected data.

Using Only Demographic Data. A midwestern state decided to assess its need for substance abuse services, to allocate funds for programs according to needs. No funds were available for the state to conduct a large study or needs assessment. The decision was made to utilize existing national and state data on those in treatment for substance abuse. These data would be used to focus on the demographic profiles of those in treatment. These profiles could be compared to the demographic characteristics of those in each county of the state. Substance abuse program funding for treatment services would be allocated to counties in proportion to the number of people fitting the profiles of substance abusers.

More Directly Relevant Secondary Data. In a second example, a substance abuse treatment program in a midsized East Coast city was informed that it needed data to justify its continued funding from the state. However, the program had neither funds nor sufficient time to conduct an assessment on the need for substance abuse services. After several calls to the city and state offices dealing with alcohol and drug abuse, it was decided that existing secondary data would provide most of the information needed. The city's health department had access to 1992 household survey data on substance use in the state. These data included sufficient numbers of participants from the city and the program's catchment area. A statistician and computer programmer from the city assisted the program to determine the prevalence and incidence rates of substance abusers in their target community. From this analysis, it was determined that the catchment area's incidence rates of drug and alcohol use for adults over the age of 25 were four times greater than those for the city. For adolescent boys, the rates were eight times greater in the target area than in the city.

The aforementioned examples involve using secondary data sources from organizations or agencies external to the one in question. However, another secondary data source that is available and sometimes useful for needs assessments is the agency's existing, routinely collected data on clients or patients. These data frequently include demographic characteristics in client or patient records, which can be used to develop profiles of clients or users of services. Those utilizing program or agency data from clients for needs assessment purposes assume that knowing about the pattern of services rendered can be useful for program planning or modifications.

The main advantage of using program-resident secondary data lies in its easy access. Also, unlike data collected on nonprogram participants, program client data are a true reflection of services rendered, not an estimate. This advantage is also its main disadvantage, however. That is, it excludes data on those who are not receiving services, but who could or should receive services. It is often the case, in fact, that human service agencies and programs underserve particular segments of their target population, such as members from dominant cultural groups. Limiting services to being mirror images of existing services means repeating the same pattern, thus limiting access by others not in the client population.

Advantages and Disadvantages. In general, the advantages of using secondary data relate to cost and time. Many representatives of public agencies have ready access to computer tapes or diskettes containing timely and relevant information that can be used easily by human service agencies and programs. Thousands of dollars go into conducting these studies to gather data that could be useful in assessing needs for services. Offices holding data useful to human service agencies include city, county, and state departments of health, education, labor/employment, substance/ drug abuse, mental health, and police as well as the voter registration, juvenile justice, and tax assessment offices. In addition to having student records, school districts commonly conduct surveys of students in their districts.

Federal offices include the Census Bureau, the Office of Substance Abuse Prevention, the Centers for Disease Control (CDC) and the National Institutes of Health, such as the National Institute on Drug Abuse, the National Institute on Mental Health, and others. Regional offices of the Census Bureau have information specialists available to help agencies and programs develop profiles of their residents that can be used in assessing service needs and planning for changes in these needs based on demographic changes.

For example, a community health clinic may want to know the proportion of residents in its catchment area who have or lack health insurance. An information specialist for the Census Bureau in a regional office can provide such an agency with insurance coverage information for even certain blocks in specific neighborhoods. Fees for such services depend on the complexity of the effort requested. However, data and assistance from public offices are generally nominal or free if already available.

Every state has state data centers that are usually affiliated with colleges or universities. These centers receive data from the Census Bureau, national health surveys, and most data from large national surveys. Even if they do not receive them, these centers have access to most federally and state sponsored data. As with the Census Bureau, these centers have statisticians and data experts who can help agencies find relevant data.

Although there are many advantages to using secondary data, there are disadvantages as well. The main disadvantage of using secondary data is that it seldom contains all of the needed information. The agency is dependent on when and about what or whom the data are collected. This limitation can be particularly troublesome for information on special segments of the population, such as dominant ethnic groups, children, adolescents, and the elderly. Latino populations are examples of groups commonly omitted from secondary data sources. Often they are included in the "Caucasion/White" racial category. Asian populations are, likewise, commonly omitted from major data collection efforts because of their smaller numbers. Moreover, Asian populations are often assumed not to have needs because of prevailing stereotypes of Asians as model minorities who lack problems and needs for educational, social, and psychological services.

Another disadvantage of secondary data is the level of technical knowledge that is sometimes needed to access and analyze it. However, this problem can be overcome by seeking assistance from the experts who are custodians of the data and whose assistance is frequently provided free or at a nominal cost. Providing assistance to human service agencies is common and sometimes even mandated by the state or federal agencies providing their funds.

Researchers from colleges and universities are also available to lend technical expertise. It is not uncommon for community-based agencies to find that researchers are conducting or have conducted research on pertinent topics and geographic areas. In such cases, researchers can provide data and offer assistance at a reasonable cost. Even if needed data are not yet available, many researchers from institutions of higher education are often eager to work with agencies to gather or collect existing data. The cost for such assistance depends on factors such as the researcher's own interest, his or her current involvement, or need for the same information and the amount of time the effort requires. In any case, researchers from colleges and universities are usually cost-effective means of obtaining data, whether secondary data or even for new needs assessments and program evaluations.

INTERVIEW METHODS

Interview methods refer to the collection of information from respondents through "real-time" face-to-face or telephone contact. Utilizing this method requires establishing rapport with respondents before querying them. Establishing rapport enables respondents to feel at ease and free to give candid responses without being concerned about criticism or disclosure. Because it requires direct contact, this method is the most time consuming and therefore the most costly, yet it can prove the most valid and comprehensive.

There are three types of interview methods: structured, semistructured, and open ended. *Structured interviews* are similar to surveys or questionnaires in that they utilize a set of specific questions with specific response choices. However, unlike most surveys, questions are typically read and responses are noted by the person administering the questionnaire (i.e., face to face contact). Below is an example of a structured question:

Over the past three months, have you considered committing suicide?

_ Yes

_ No

_ Not Sure

Structured questions can be read to the respondent or read and shown in writing. Regardless, it is recommended that the range of response choices be given in writing. In this way respondents, particularly those that are more visually oriented, can thoroughly consider the range of responses.

Semistructured interview methods refer to the use of questions that offer a fixed set of response choices but leave one or more unrestricted responses open to respondents to write in their own words. Consider the following example:

What is your race or ethnicity?

____   Hispanic/Latino
         Specify Subgroup: _____

____   African American

____   Anglo/White

____   Native American/American Indian
         Specify Subgroup: _____

____   Asian
         Specify Subgroup: _____

____   Other:_____
         _____
         _____
         _____

This example offers predetermined *fixed options* (choices), while providing *open-ended* or unrestricted opportunities to respond. As with structured questions, interviewers may simply read the question and response choices to respondents or they may read the question and show participants the response options. Some people may ask, why not just omit all choices and let respondents write their own responses? There are two main reasons for offering semistructured items like the one above. First, this type of question makes it easier and faster for respondents to respond since viable and presumeably likely responses are offered. Second, providing fixed options helps respondents consider the full range of responses, thereby helping them select the best and most valid answer, instead of choosing the first choice that comes to mind. In general, the main advantage of using the semistructured interview method centers on providing respondents with viable or realistic and convenient response choices that they can select expediently, while allowing for unique responses to fall outside of the fixed choices.

Disadvantages of semistructured questions include the likelihood that respondents will chose from among the fixed options when perhaps a more accurate response does not fit listed responses adequately. Research experience shows that respondents tend to chose from among fixed-choice options out of convenience and expediency. As a result, responses to questions using fixed choices may only reveal approximations of true or more valid responses. Social desirability, the desire to answer questions as others do, is a strong desire among many respondents. At times they interpret fixed-choice response options as "normal" or socially sanctioned.

Open-ended or *unstructured questions* have no restrictions for respondents. An example of such a question is:

What do you think are concerns some people might have about putting a residential program for the mentally retarded on your block?

This question allows respondents to consider reasons for and against a specific proposal, thought, feeling, condition, or idea without constraints. Moreover, open-ended questions allow responses to be complete and qualified in the words of the respondent, not the interviewer. With such questions, interviewers also have the opportunity to ask respondents to clarify and expound on responses and reasons for them. Using such questions results in a greater range of more complete responses.

The main advantage of open-ended questions is the qualitative nature of the answers. Fuller, more detailed responses often provide their context. Disadvantages to open-ended questions include the greater amount of time needed to code the responses. There is also the risk that the responses will not be easy to code. Because of the more elaborate nature of these data, information from open-ended questionnaires does not lend itself readily to quantification. The focus of these questions is primarily on their descriptive and qualitative nature.

Within structured, semistructured, and open-ended interview methods, respondents are questioned face to face. Although these methods were considered independently, they can be fruitfully used in combination in a single needs assessment. Human service providers may feel that some issues can be best queried using structured questions, but other issues may be handled best without restrictions to responses. Any of these methods can be used on a variety of populations. The application of any of these face-to-face methods on a select group of particularly knowledgeable respondents is called the key informant method, which we will now consider.

KEY INFORMANT METHOD

The use of the key informant method for needs assessments presupposes the existence of a select group of people who hold or have access to most, if not all, of the information needed to evaluate a target population. In using the key informant method, researchers commonly select agency representatives and/or community leaders. Suppose, for example, that a city is interested in knowing about the specific concerns and problems related to housing, mental health, and substance abuse to determine the service needs related to these issues in the city. Using the key informant method, community agency representatives and community leaders from the area could be selected, based on their expertise and working relationship with the community, to describe, explicate, and enumerate concerns in the relevant subject areas. In this example, directors of local housing programs, mental health centers, and substance-abuse treatment centers, among other relevant community leaders, would be interviewed for their opinions. Among the advantages of key informant groups is the ability of participants to competently address specific topics.

An important advantage of the key informant method lies in the limited number of participants needed, because key informants are presumed to have a broad knowledge of needs within the targeted area. The main disadvantage is its reliance on a small number of participants who, for several reasons, may be biased in their perceptions. A common mistake is to exclude community leaders and residents who, although they may not hold public office or paid positions, hold key information about the community and its needs from their everyday interaction with residents. By focusing exclusively on the agency representatives who provide services for relevant issues, one runs the risk of obtaining information that maintains the status quo. That is, agency representatives have the tendency to justify the availability of current services. Hence, the community problems and concerns revealed may be only those for which services exist.

Key informants are interviewed either individually or in groups. (Any of the previously mentioned interviewing methods can be used with the key informant method.) A particularly effective method of querying respondents in small groups is called the focus group method.

FOCUS GROUPS

The use of focus groups for determining human service needs has been increasing in popularity and use in the human services field. For years, focus groups have been used by marketing firms to assess product needs and develop marketing strategies and product evaluation. Only recently has this methodology been used in the human service fields. Focus groups usually consist of eight to ten participants and a moderator or facilitator. However, sometimes even smaller groups of five to seven respondents are preferred, because they allow individual group members to participate more.

Optimal meeting times range from 40 minutes to three hours, depending on the breadth and depth of topics. To avoid participant fatigue, it is not recommended that groups meet for more than three hours at a time. A particular strength of focus groups is their concentration on the quality, not the quantity, of information. That is, the method offers participants an opportunity to express their views with no response restrictions. Consequently, participants typically become engaged in the topics at a greater level.

Selecting Participants. As with any small group or sample, the particular participants selected will determine the representation of the group's responses to broader populations. Focus groups work best when researchers seek the views of select or homogeneous subpopulations. For example, a family planning organization may want to conduct a focus group on sexually active teenage females to find out the best methods of informing them of the risks of contracting HIV infection and AIDS through unprotected sex. This group may feel that ethnic minority adolescent females are particularly hard to inform, so a focus group involving such representatives may be important.

In general, what is gained in in-depth and comprehensive information is lost in broad representation when using focus groups for needs assessments. Understanding who the participants are and what groups they represent is the key to interpreting and generalizing the outcome of focus groups. It may be conceptually appealing to run focus groups with diverse participants differing socially and/or culturally. However, facilitators face great challenges in running groups with participants holding diverse views.

There are exceptions, however, to discouraging diverse membership within focus groups. One is when differences in opinion on discussion topics are not expected to generate hostility or conflict and when diverse opinions add to the breadth of opinions needed. For example, a "Parents as Teachers" program may want to conduct a focus group with culturally diverse mothers better to understand common barriers keeping mothers from interacting with their children. Unless the group lacks sensitivity and acceptance, having culturally diverse mothers would add to the breadth of understanding of mother-child interactions. Another example is when conflict between members of different groups is the actual focus of the information sought. A group composed of police officers and community residents who misunderstand and mistrust each other is an example of a group whose conflict can in fact be the focus of discussion in a focus group. Such a focus group could center on identifying methods of increasing trust and communication between police and communities.

Focus Group Discussion Guide. The facilitator or discussion moderator typically prepares a subject guide, a list of topics or questions that are to be discussed during the time allotted. Below is an example of such a guide used in a focus group on gang membership and violence among adolescents. Preceding the guide is an introduction made by the facilitator before beginning the discussion. An introduction is important for setting the guidelines and expectations for the discussion.

FOCUS GROUP DISCUSSION GUIDE ON GANGS AND VIOLENCE TOPICS AND POSSIBLE QUESTIONS TO ASK

You have all read and signed consent forms, which explained the reason for these discussions and gave you the choice of volunteering or not volunteering to take part in them. Remember, we will not tell anyone you have participated in these discussions. You do not have to be in these discussions and you can leave the discussion at any time you feel uncomfortable.

Even though I have many questions and topics I want us to discuss in the next hour and a half, I hope that you will feel free to give your views at any time. No one person should be the focus of this discussion. Each of you has valuable opinions that are important to listen to. There are no right or wrong answers to any of the topics discussed or questions asked. It is important that each of us respect all views expressed even if we don't agree with them. We need to agree to disagree. It is important that everyone have a chance to talk during our discussion.

Before starting, does anyone have any questions? If not, let us start by introducing ourselves to each other. I'll start with myself.

General Topical Questions
Why gangs?
Why violence?

Family
What about families and gangs?
What about families and violence?

Parents
What about parents?

Family Functioning
What about family problems?

Peer Influence
What about peers?

Discrimination/Prejudice
What about discrimination and prejudice?

Schools
What about schools?

Economics and Jobs
What about income and jobs?

Substance Use
What about drugs and alcohol?

Services for Youth Gangs and Violence
What about services for youth gangs and violent offenders?

96-592

There are several important things about this guide. First is its intent to develop rapport and a trusting relationship with participants. Personal introductions help to serve this purpose, as do assurances of confidentiality. Second, the list provides an outline of categories of topics about which the researcher is interested in seeking opinions and views. Researchers sometimes simply use these categories with no questions listed under them. However, in this case the researcher has listed subjects she would like covered. These subjects are not formed as questions, but are proposed as general themes. The queries go from questions to general themes. The participants quickly learn that the role of the facilitator is simply to guide the discussion, but not to dictate specific questions or responses. This strategy is both freeing and challenging for the researcher, because the discussion can easily veer off the relevant topics or delve too much into one to the exclusion of others.

Without such guides, facilitators may find that important topics are not discussed. Although facilitators help guide the discussion, they do not impose great restrictions on it. That is, the information sought from focus groups should go beyond posing restricted or concrete questions to more open-ended questions. For example, the question, "Do you feel your local police department is doing enough to fight crime in your neighborhood?," may lead to short responses like "yes," "no," and "I think so," but stifle in-depth discussion. Instead, it is preferable for facilitators to present topics instead of direct questions.

Although facilitators should not be directive or imposing, they need to ensure that group discussions cover the range of topics of importance. This requirement means facilitators need to facilitate transitions between topics. For example, a facilitator may help make the transition from an engaging discussion for 30 minutes on the promotion in high schools of the use of condoms by saying: "We have heard many important and valid views on this critical and engaging topic. What about the role of parents in discussing sexual topics with their children?"

In this example the facilitator first validated all previous responses then posed an open-ended question redirecting the discussion. As mentioned earlier, closed-ended questions cut off or stifle discussion.

Recording and Coding Focus Group Responses. Conducting focus groups almost always requires recording the sessions on audiotape to free group facilitators from having to keep notes on group discussions and to refer to when reporting results. Audiorecordings, however, require that researchers secure written permission from participants to record them. Researchers should also make sure to test the audio equipment, making sure that it is sensitive enough to record low-level voices.

A big challenge to using a focus group methodology is knowing how to summarize the outcome of focus groups. Typically, a lot of in-depth discussions take place on a wide range of related topics, but the researcher has to decipher the overall outcome of these group discussions. To address this need, the researcher must refer to the purpose of the study and to the key questions forming the basis of the needs assessment (see Chapter 1). Sticking to these questions and not allowing irrelevant deviations will help the researcher overcome the temptation to record all interesting information from discussions.

Unlike quantitative methods, focus groups provide qualitative information. Their strength is in-depth and comprehensive coverage of subject areas. Hence the reporting of the results should reflect this strength. List the key questions with the consensus of respondents to them. Recording the overall consensus of participants is critical; however, noting deviations from consensus, particularly those coming from members of special populations (e.g., gender, age, ethnicity/race, educational background, income, regional background, culture, religion). If responses from such subpopulations are important, their responses should be clearly noted and contrasted. If their views are important enough, then perhaps a focus group only on them is warranted.

Advantages and Disadvantages. Information derived from focus groups can stand on its own merits or be combined with existing quantitative data on the same topics. For example, companies interested in marketing a laundry detergent may already know the size of their market, but may need more in-depth information about the criteria used when selecting a detergent. Similarly, a community mental-health center may have convincing data (such as divorce rates) showing the need for family therapy in a particular minority community. However, because of the historically low participation rates in this community, focus groups may be used more clearly to illuminate the reasons for the community's reluctance to participate in family therapy. It is possible, for example, for focus groups to reveal specific barriers to service use as well as to point out particular counseling needs that a mental health center needs to provide to minority populations.

Focus groups can also be utilized to collect information needed to design more quantitative needs assessment instruments. If conducted correctly, focus groups provide very rich and comprehensive information that more structured methods, such as surveys or questionnaires, cannot provide. Because of the specific focus of this technique, the results derived can have a profound impact on program or organizational operations. For focus groups to be used effectively in research, however, enough groups need to be conducted to reflect the diversity of the targeted population. For example, separate focus groups may be organized by education, occupation, gender, culture, socioeconomic status, etc., depending on the saliency of these characteristics and their importance to the human services in question.

There are two important limitations of focus groups. One is the strict emphasis on qualitative or descriptive data. That is, focus group information cannot be numerically quantified or scaled in coding. Even within focus groups, one cannot use proportions or numerical representations (e.g., 20% of the focus group did not see a need for such-and-such services), as these statistics are highly influenced by a few individuals and can therefore be misleading. Another important weakness of the technique is its reliance on the facilitator to run the group properly, with no subjective interference, and to be objective in reporting the findings.

The reader is referred to several publications for further information on the use of focus groups (e.g., Debus & Porter, 1989).

EXERCISES

This chapter has reviewed commonly used needs assessment methods, such as existing data—secondary data sources—interview, key informant, and focus group methods. Knowing which method to use depends on the information needs and the time and resources available. The following exercises will help the reader develop a greater sensitivity to factors dictating the appropriateness of one method over another for particular applications.

Four scenarios are presented below. Chose the most appropriate needs assessment method for each. There is one vignette for each method discussed in this chapter. Bear in mind that most needs assessments can be successfully accomplished using any of several assessment methods. However, presenting circumstances, such as financial, people or time constraints, often dictates the appropriateness of one method over another. The answers are listed at the end of the chapter.

VIGNETTE ONE:
Community Health Clinic

A community health clinic has been providing primary care for more than 40 years in a culturally diverse neighborhood of about equal proportions of Latinos, African Americans, and Asians. However, this clinic has traditionally catered to the needs of Latinos to the exclusion of African

Americans and Asians. This bias was never the intention of the clinic and has been an admitted embarrassment to it. Asians and African Americans have traditionally had their health care needs met at a local county hospital. Funding cuts at the hospital for indigent care, coupled with increased opportunities for funding in community-based clinics that demonstrate significant increases in services for multicultural populations, have led the clinic to conduct a needs assessment of the African American and Asian populations.

A special fundraising event undertaken to support the needs assessment generated $8,000. Most of this money was used to free up 50% of the time of one clinical social worker in the clinic who was finishing her doctorate. The health clinic is one of 27 community-based organizations strongly rooted in this culturally diverse population. The 27 agencies are equally divided in their affiliation with the three ethnic populations in the neighborhood. The heads of these agencies are considered leaders knowledgeable about their respective ethnic communities. Moreover, each ethnic group has strong attachments to churches whose ministers are leaders tied to specific ethnic populations in the neighborhood.

The following purpose and key questions were accepted and used to guide the needs assessment by the health clinic:

Purpose: To identify salient barriers keeping African Americans and Asians from seeking health services in the clinic.

Key Questions: Regarding African American and Asian communities:

1. What perceptions do members of these ethnic communities have of:
   - The clinic
   - Its staff
   - Its services
2. What are salient barriers to people seeking services from the clinic?

Which method is most appropriate given the circumstances? (Choose one.)

_____ Secondary Data Method

_____ Interview Method

_____ Key Informant Method

_____ Focus Group Method

Why did you choose this needs assessment method? Explain:

_____

_____

_____

_____

VIGNETTE TWO:
Gang Mediation

A gang mediation program in a West Coast city has been asked by its funders to become more involved in meeting the broader counseling needs of gang members related to their family, income, and educational status. It was thought that a needs assessment focusing on problem areas within these realms would point out specific barriers to their integration in society and thus areas for counseling. The gang mediation program's target population is in the west side of a midsized city that has clear, established geographic boundaries. Gang members in the neighborhood belong to one of three gangs who have clear boundaries in the same neighborhood.

The following purpose and key questions were adopted for the needs assessment:

Purpose: To determine counseling needs related to family, income, and education.

Key Questions:

1. To assess gang members' concerns related to their:
   - Relationship with family
   - Education and job training
   - Income and job status
2. To identify barriers to acceptance of counseling services within these subject realms by gang members.
3. Perceived need and effectiveness of current gang mediation.

Which method is most appropriate given the circumstances? (Choose one.)

_____ Secondary Data Method

_____ Interview Method

_____ Key Informant Method

_____ Focus Group Method

Why did you choose this needs assessment method? Explain:

_____

_____

_____

_____

VIGNETTE THREE:
A National Preschool Preparation Program—
How to Spend Increased Program Funding
(This scenario is hypothetical.)

Over the past several years, a national preschool program has been granted a significant funding increase because of its success in enhancing the academic and intellectual preparation of preschool children for school. How should the program expand its services to affect a greater number of children? It is recognized that a needs assessment is necessary to expand services. However, whatever assessment is chosen must be national in scope. Unfortunately, the agency does not have funding allocated for a needs assessment nor does it have personnel with time available to devote to the task. However, a foundation was willing to provide up to $5,000 to the agency for information-gathering tasks. After several meetings, it was decided that a needs assessment would be conducted that focused on the following purpose and key questions:

Purpose: To identify underserved populations.

Key Questions:

1. What subpopulations are underserved?
2. What are the social and cultural characteristics of underserved populations?
3. Why are they underserved?
4. Based on the preceding information, generate a list of recommendations to remove barriers.
5. Make recommendations about areas of program expansion.

Which method is most appropriate given the circumstances? (Choose one.)

_____ Secondary Data Method

_____ Interview Method

_____ Key Informant Method

_____ Focus Group Method

Why did you choose this needs assessment method? Explain:

_____

_____

_____

_____

VIGNETTE FOUR:
Battered Women's Program

A relatively new battered women's program launched a media effort to inform the public about the crippling effect of physical abuse on women in a small southern city. This information campaign was also meant to let women know about the shelter. Although many radio and television stations carried the shelter's message, relatively few women came to the shelter for assistance. Instead, battered women continued to rely on hospitals for treatment before returning to their partners or relying on friends and family for temporary shelter.

The program decided that it lacked the information to explain this underutilization. The program had to rely on its own resources to conduct a needs assessment. The director decided to undertake the assessment with the help of one of the program's social workers. The following purpose and key questions were decided:

Purpose: To determine why battered women do not seek assistance from the program and shelter.

Key Questions:

1. How informed are battered women about the program and shelter?
2. What barriers prevent battered women from utilizing the program's services?
3. What suggestions do battered women have to overcome barriers to usage of the program's services?

Which method is most appropriate given the circumstances? (Choose one.)

____ Secondary Data Method

____ Interview Method

____ Key Informant Method

____ Focus Group Method

Why did you choose this needs assessment method? Explain:

_____

_____

_____

_____

ANSWERS
Vignette One

After paying for a half-time staff member, not much money remains to undertake a comprehensive survey of the community. Choosing the interview method would require too many residents for one person to interview. Furthermore, the particular staff person has more training in therapy than in conducting research. Hence, conducting a quantitative study is not feasible. With focus group methodology, selecting sufficiently representative participants from the relevant subpopulations would be a problem (i.e., age, gender, family roles, and so on). Therefore, the most prudent choice is the key informant method, because there are strong and plentiful community leaders who have intimate knowledge of their respective ethnic communities.

Vignette Two

Conducting a traditional impersonal survey with gang members, as with delinquents, is not very successful given their social alienation and mistrust of others outside their gang. Nor would a focus group methodology work because a code of honor dictates little fraternizing with those outside of the gang, especially with those gang members call "suits" (government or agency representatives). The key informant method is not attractive, because those who could be considered key informants have had little contact with or knowledge of gang members. Finally, no secondary data are available specific to gang members, particularly those in their area.

The interview method was selected because it allowed interviewers to talk to individual gang members and to develop rapport with them before asking them about their counseling needs. Open-ended questions were used because they offered the least restriction on gang members' responses.

Vignette Three

Conducting a needs assessment using secondary data is best for various reasons. For one, there was little money or personnel available to conduct an assessment. Second, the needs assessment needed to be national in scope, which necessitated using national data. It is unrealistic to gather new data at the national level with such limited funds. Many useful secondary data sources can help guide this program. For one, the program would do well to gather whatever data it has on those they currently serve, listing out demographics and other characteristics. This information can be used to develop a profile of current users, which can be compared to the demographics of cities where programs are located. This comparison would point to underserved populations, whether they are selected on income, ethnicity/race, age or family structure, or other factors.

To understand barriers for services, consult the literature on patterns and barriers to service underutilization by people such as the group identified. For example, there is a significant body of literature and research on the underutilization of mental health services by ethnic or racial minorities, which could be used to identify common service barriers. Recommendations for service expansion can be made based on secondary data sources. It is important to recognize that the best method to choose under financial and resource constraints does not mean that the method chosen will provide the required information. It is not uncommon, for example, for large agencies with significant program funding to skimp on needs assessments or program evaluation, only to find out that they failed to provide adequate services to everyone in their target area.

Vignette Four

Only internal resources are available to the organization to conduct a needs assessment, which suggests the needs assessment will be limited in its number of participants (i.e., excludes a survey). The target population is a select group composed of battered women or those at risk. The key informant method is not chosen, because other agency representatives and community leaders are not knowledgeable enough about the problem and its victims. Although interviews with battered women may prove helpful, the limited time the staff has makes this method inefficient.

No secondary data exist that focus on the targeted area or the program's failed efforts to draw clients. Conducting focus groups of battered and at-risk women was the method of choice because of its efficiency and ability to query women in a supportive group environment. Referrals for the focus group came from the county hospital and department of social services.

Chapter 3

SURVEY METHODS AND
SAMPLE SIZE REQUIREMENTS

"At last night's meeting, what kind of needs assessment did the board suggest we conduct for the center?," Leticia asked. Paul answered, "They didn't 'suggest,' they *mandated* that we conduct a survey."

"A survey?," she cried. "Well, did they tell you how to conduct one?"

"No. They didn't even think we would need help. They told us that conducting a survey was the easiest way to do a needs assessment, because everyone hears about survey results all the time."

"But, Paul," Leticia replied worriedly, "we don't know anything about surveys! Where do we start? How many people do we need for a survey?"

Indeed, we often read about surveys being conducted or sponsored by many groups and organizations. They are so common that it would appear that surveys are easy for anyone to conduct. Surveys are certainly among the most commonly selected methods for conducting needs assessments because surveys can very easily and expediently generate a significant amount of numerical or quantitative data. At the same time, however, their apparent convenience masks their inherent complexity, which makes them one of the most misused data collection methods. Furthermore, problems also occurr with the interpretation and reporting of survey results.

Still, surveys can be appropriately and effectively used in conducting needs assessments for several reasons. One, surveys are a cost-effective means of collecting information from a large numbers of individuals, often with little assistance given to participants when responding. Because surveys can be efficiently administered to large numbers of respondents, surveys are more likely to provide results that are representative of the target population. Quantifying responses, such as attitudes, perceptions, and needs for services, is an important attribute of this method. Other methods, such as interview methods, can also yield quantitative results. However, surveys are better able to do so because they rely largely on fixed-choice questions.

There is no one preferred survey method to use when conducting needs assessments. Surveys come in different forms: mailout surveys (e.g., questionnaires), telephone surveys, or face-to-face surveys. When questionnaires are used, they are typically structured or at least semistructured. Generally, the larger the sample or number of participants in the survey, the greater the reliance on structured or fixed-choice questions. Fixed-choice questions allow responses to be tabulated quickly and the wide range of possible responses from mixed or open-ended questions requires the development of elaborate coding schemes to encompass most of the possible responses.

Funders and other external stakeholders often prefer quantitative results, which surveys provide, because numbers suggest a quantity of an attribute being measured, whether an opinion, need, perception, belief, or preference. Moreover, this quantified attribute can be compared to that of another area, a national estimate, or to the same area but at a different time.

As with other methods, scope and content requirements continue to be determined by the sponsoring organization, other stakeholders, and the resources and time available. Issues such as the data collection method and sampling requirements need to be considered before undertaking a needs assessment using survey methods.

DATA COLLECTION METHODS

As mentioned earlier, a first step in conducting a needs assessment is to outline the issues the assessment will address. For example, the question, "How many adolescents between the ages of 12 and 16 are addicted to illegal substances in the city?" requires a more sophisticated and detailed survey method than the question, "Do adolescents between the ages of 12 and 16 need substance abuse services?" The latter question imposes fewer numerical requirements and offers the researcher more latitude in defining a need for substance abuse services.

Surveys can use any of the different types of interview methods discussed earlier, such as structured, semistructured, open-ended, or unstructured methods. Structured, or fixed-choice, questions are favored for quantitatively focused surveys. The question, "How many cigarettes do you smoke per day?" is an example of a very structured question with a numerical focus. Unstructured or open-ended questions are typically used more to answer "why" questions than "how much" or "how many" questions. The questions needing to be answered will determine whether to use open or fixed-choice questions.

With both structured and open-ended questions, pretesting the questions on a small sample of respondents is imperative to ensure that questions are understood and interpreted in the same way across subjects and that the response options offered truly capture the range of preferred choices. After determining the type and number of questions needed, sample selection and size become important.

SAMPLE SELECTION METHODS

Organizations conducting needs assessments must determine their target population. This is one of the most neglected requirements of any study. Knowing the geographic boundaries and specific characteristics of the target population are imperative. For example, a senior citizen's recreational center that desires to assess the interest in and likely participation of seniors in center-organized trips to Las Vegas would ideally want to select a sample of all eligible senior citizens in its catchment area. But if the agency can only serve seniors earning under a certain annual income, a study including all senior citizens may lead to inappropriate estimates of future program participants. To avoid this problem, agencies need to have very clear inclusion and exclusion criteria for a study that reflect a clear perception of the target population.

Inclusion criteria relate to basic characteristics that participants must have to be a part of the survey. A middle school mentoring program may, for example, want to conduct a survey of low-income minority middle schoolers between the ages of 11 and 14 who live in a particular public housing complex and come from single-parent households. In this example, there are five inclusion criteria: (a) income, (b) age, (c) school status (whether in school), (d) family structure, and (e) housing location—six, if you add (f) neighborhood residence.

One might say, "Easy enough, the exclusion criteria are those not fitting the inclusion criteria." True, but noting specific exclusion criteria is also helpful for eliminating confounding variables. Confounding variables are factors or population characteristics that can mislead in interpretation of the results. Let us say we used the preceding inclusion criteria and conducted a survey of selected respondents about their attitudes toward mentoring and being mentored.

Without adequate exclusion criteria, researchers may find the selected sample consists of two or more subpopulations. For example, the sample may consist of people from families who are committed to criminal activity (selling drugs, heavily using drugs, or engaging in other serious criminal activities) and those economically struggling, but trying to help their children succeed. The first group's strong commitment to illegal activity, desire for anonymity, and fear of disclosure may lead to a resounding "no" by its members to an offer of outside intervention or relationship building. On the other hand, the second group may be more open to and interested in mentoring. Averaging interest in mentoring of both groups may result in overall lukewarm interest in mentoring and hide the two group's differing opinions. In this case, commitment to illegal activity becomes a confounding variable affecting the final interpretation of the study. Knowing early about such possible confounding variables may help researchers look for subpopulations in a sample or develop exclusion criteria to eliminate subpopulations not of interest to the program or organization conducting the needs assessment.

SIMPLE RANDOM METHOD

Once the target population has been clearly defined, the method of selecting study participants needs to be decided. Empirically, the preferred method of subject selection is called the simple random method. It involves having a list of all in the target population and selecting a random sample from it. In a true random sampling, each person on this comprehensive list would have an equal probability of being selected as part of the sample. Most statistical books include a table of random numbers that can be used to select the survey participants. However, rarely do agencies or researchers have a complete listing of individuals from their target populations. This requires the use of alternative sampling methods that work around this limitation.

In practice, the simple random method is used more in program evaluation than in conducting needs assessments. However, target populations are sometimes accessible enough to use the simple random sample method. Consider, for example, a needs assessment of the educational, occupational and recreational needs among resident youth in California Youth Authority's (CYA) many residential camps and holding facilities. A complete listing of those in the target population—youth wards—can be easily obtained to select at random 1,000 youth for the needs assessment. Using the simple random procedures would lead to a truly representative sample reflective of all wards living in CYA's residential facilities. However, in many cases complete lists of those in targeted populations are either not possible, too costly or too difficult to obtain. Even so, when when possible, the simple random method should be considered the method of choice for conducting a needs assessment.

CONVENIENCE SAMPLING METHODS

One widely used method for subject selection when simple random selection is not possible is called the convenience sample selection method, also called the nonrandom selection technique. This sample selection method takes into consideration the availability of participants in the study. It involves, as the term implies, selecting a convenient and accessible sample using whatever eligible respondents are available to the researcher. Obviously the appropriateness of a convenience sample depends on its representation of the target population. Its appropriateness can range from totally justified to absolutely inadequate.

Commonly used are five convenient sampling techniques: (a) quota, (b) interval, (c) judgment, (d) systematic, and (e) snowball. The following section examines each of these techniques to clarify their differences.

Quota Sampling Method. The quota sampling method involves deciding on a fixed number of subjects with particular characteristics. For example, a health clinic may decide to interview 25 male and 25 female patients from the clinic. It could use the first 25 male and the first 25 female patients coming in the clinic or the first five patients in each of five days. The problem with this method is that patients selected during a particular time of the day may not represent all patients.

For example, pregnant women may be more likely to be chosen because perhaps during the time participants are chosen the prenatal clinic offers special screenings. Alternatively, nonworking patients may be overrepresented in quota samples if they are selected during morning hours. To avoid such biases in quota selection, researchers may decide to choose days and times randomly for the selection of survey participants.

Interval Sampling Method. The interval sampling method involves the selection of subjects in periodic sequence. Using the previous gender selection example, instead of selecting the first 25 men, a health clinic could use the interval sampling method and select every eighth male patient coming in. The interval sampling method can also be used to draw a series of samples over time. For example, patient satisfaction can be measured on a monthly basis over a specified time period such as a year.

As with other methods, researchers need to be sensitive to possible selection biases resulting from following rigid or specified patterns of data collection. For example, choosing the first day of every month to conduct a needs assessment may preselect participants available on that particular day (e.g., employed people who visit the clinic on the first of the month because it is payday).

The interval method is an important way of selecting participants from a convenience population. Used wisely, it helps select a more representative sample of the target population than otherwise possible. The interval sampling method's main weakness lies in its misuse, selecting nonrepresentative samples by relying on rigid and patterned selection criteria (e.g., selecting every fifth person up to 50—when it is known that the first 100 people are nonrepresentative of the broader target population—for example, one gender only).

Systematic Sampling Method. A common sampling method is called the systematic sampling method, which is used to select subjects from very large populations. For example, a researcher may be interested in selecting a representative sample of listed telephone users from Albuquerque, New Mexico, by using a telephone directory. Rather than choosing a sample at random, a researcher can divide the number of phone numbers in the directory by the number of subjects needed and, using this number as *n*, select every *n*th subject from the listing. The starting point is usually randomly selected. This method is the closest to the simple random method and is expected to yield similar results.

Judgment Sampling Method. The judgment sampling method focuses on using the knowledge of experts to select a sample of participants representative of the targeted population. This method can be particularly useful in studies focusing on very narrow subpopulations. For example, psychiatrists specializing in schizophrenia can use their experience with patients to select cases typical of most schizophrenics for a study on the common behavioral patterns of schizophrenics. The disadvantage of this method is its strict reliance on the subjective judgment of experts, which may prove biased or nonrepresentative.

Snowball Sampling Method. The snowball method, a convenient sampling technique, entails starting with a small group of accessible subjects and using them to recruit others who also meet the selection criteria for the study. The snowball method has two main advantages over a simpler convenient sample method. The careful selection of the initial small group can lead to a more representative sample. The snowball method can also result in higher participation rates among those recruited, because study participants generally recruit others whom they know and can convince to participate. The snowball method is particularly useful when a researcher needs difficult-to-find samples, such as gang members.

The validity and reliability of a study are directly influenced by the representativeness of the sample from the target population. The most empirically sound sample selection method is the true random selection method. However, as mentioned, this method is often not practical and/or too costly. This is not to say that a convenience sample is never needed, appropriate, or useful. However, the adequacy of a convenient sample depends on the appropriate inclusion or representation of members of the target population. Generally the smaller, narrower, and more distinct the target population is, the more likely a convenience sample will adequately represent the target population. Conversely, the larger and more diverse the targeted population, the more likely a large and diverse sample is needed.

As an example of the appropriateness of convenience samples, consider how a convenience sample of crack abusing, Anglo male adolescent prostitutes in Kansas City is likely to represent crack abusing, Anglo male adolescent prostitutes in the United States. In this case, a convenience sample may work fine. Now consider a convenience sample of the same size of married Anglo female parents from Kansas City. Would this convenience sample be representative of all married Anglo female parents in the United States? Unlikely, because the target population is so large and diverse. This fact decreases the likelihood of successfully selecting a representative sample using a convenience sample method. It is important to note that very rigorous random selection procedures are in fact often used with methods we here label convenience methods, which can lead to acquiring samples as representative of a target population as those derived using the simple random method.

In general, the sample selection method chosen will mainly depend on the available resources (i.e., financial, staff, and time) and access to members of the target population. Needs assessments are often conducted at the request of a program funder, a parent organization, or the program itself. Determining specific internal and external organizational expectations regarding the scope and empirical accuracy of a needs assessment is very important before initiating efforts. Also critical is a serious consideration of the sample size.

SAMPLE SIZE REQUIREMENTS

How many subjects are enough? This is the ever-troublesome question facing researchers conducting a study. Unfortunately, the answer is not clear cut. As with sampling selection strategies, resource availability is one of the most significant factors determining sample size. Still, another critical factor is the specific focus of the study; that is, the key questions the agency wants the needs assessment to answer. For example, it is one thing to want to know the proportion of people from a particular community who drink excessively; it is another to want to know the proportions of those who demonstrate the same behavior by gender, ethnicity, and socioeconomic subgroup.

On a technical level, sample size depends on two main factors other than cost: the desired accuracy of the attribute(s) being measured and the variation or heterogeneity of the population in respect to that attribute(s). The accuracy of a result or statistic, such as a percent, is referred to as *sampling error.* Sampling error is a statistic or percentage that estimates the accuracy of the sample parameter or statistic. For example, if 50% of a sample of married Latino male professionals used condoms for contraception, and the sampling error were 3%, we could assume that the true population parameter is between minus or plus 3% around the sample estimate of 50% (i.e., 47% to 53%). Sampling errors of 3% to 5% are commonly accepted.

A *confidence level* is another important statistic that indicates the confidence one can place in the accuracy of the sampling error. In the preceding example, a 95% confidence level would suggest that one can be 95% confident that the true population parameter or statistic is between plus and minus the derived sampling error. Normal confidence rates are 95% or 99%.

Deriving confidence levels and sampling errors involves using complex statistical formulas. However, statistical tables available in good survey sampling books simplify determining sample sizes. Table 3.1 is an example of a table that can be used to determine sample sizes depending on the sampling error desired. As the table shows, the sampling error is not reduced appreciably by having a sample of more than 2,000. A general principle in sampling is that the adequacy of sample size is not dependent on the size of the target population. The only exception is when the sample is more than 10% of the population. In such cases, a smaller sample size is equally accurate.

To illustrate the use of Table 3.1, let us say that a drug detoxification program wants to conduct a needs assessment of the local community's hearing and comprehension of public service announcements (PSA) that the agency promoted on a popular radio station over the previous year. These PSAs were targeted at parents of adolescents to inform them of the dangers of drug abuse, their role in helping their children avoid drugs, and the existence of the detoxification program. For this needs assessment, the targeted population are parents of adolescents.

TABLE 3.1 Sample Sizes Required for Various Sampling Errors at 95%
Confidence Level (Simple Random Sampling)

Sampling Error[a] Percentage	Sample Size[b]	Sampling Error	Sample Size
1.0	10,000	5.5	330
1.5	4,500	6.0	277
2.0	2,500	6.5	237
2.5	1,600	7.0	204
3.0	1,100	7.5	178
3.5	816	8.0	156
4.0	625	8.5	138
4.5	494	9.0	123
5.0	400	9.5	110
		10.0	100

SOURCE: de Vaus, D. A. (1990). *Surveys in social research* (2nd ed., p. 7). Boston, MA: George Allen & Unwin. Reprinted by permission.
NOTES: a. This is in fact two standard errors (+ & –).
b. This assumes a 50/50 split on the variable. These sample sizes would be smaller for more homogeneous samples.

The important estimate sought through this assessment is the proportion of parents in one community who had heard and understood the messages of the PSAs. If the detoxification program wanted responses to this and other questions and could get only 100 parents to participate, how accurate or reflective would the proportion or statistic be of the entire population? Table 3.1 demonstrates that 100 respondents would provide responses or results that can deviate from the "true" response by around 10%. So for example, if 55% of the sample said they had heard and understood the PSA announcements, we can be 95% (confidence level) sure that the "true" proportion (if we included all parents of adolescents from the area in the survey) would lie somewhere between 45% and 65% of the population. Table 3.1 also shows that quadrupling the sample to 400 cuts the potential measurement error in half.

Optimal sample sizes also depend on the heterogeneity of the largest population and on the level of agreement in responding to questions. That is, the use of Table 3.1 is appropriate when the responses to key questions are expected to be equally distributed across response choices. For example, in a true/false question, 50% of respondents would chose true and 50% would chose false. This proportion means there is heterogeneity in the sample as reflected in the responses. However, sometimes the responses are expected to be lopsided or homogeneous, as when 10% select true and 90% select false. Generally, the more unified or homogeneous the population, the smaller the number required in a sample. Table 3.2

TABLE 3.2 Required Sample Sizes Depending on Population Homogeneity
and Desired Accuracy

Acceptable Sampling Error[a]	Percentage of Population Expected to Give Particular Answer					
	5/95	10/90	20/80	30/70	40/60	50/50
1%	1900	3600	6400	8400	9600	10,000
2%	479	900	1600	2100	2400	2,500
3%	211	400	711	933	1066	1,100
4%	119	225	400	525	600	625
5%	76	144	256	336	370	400
6%	—[b]	100	178	233	267	277
7%	—	73	131	171	192	204
8%	—	—	100	131	150	156
9%	—	—	79	104	117	123
10%	—	—	—	84	96	100

SOURCE: de Vaus, D. A. (1990). *Surveys in social research* (2nd ed., p. 72). Boston, MA:
George Allen & Unwin. Reprinted by permission.
NOTES: a. At the 95% level of confidence
b. Samples smaller than this would normally be too small for meaningful analysis.

represents the types of tables that take expected variability of responses
into account (i.e., heterogeneity/homogeneity).

Table 3.2 shows sample size requirements for different levels of agreement in responding to needs assessment questions. For example, consider
the following question and response options presented to a sample of retired residents of a particular city:

**Bus trips to Las Vegas and other gambling cities should be scheduled once
a month for those of us who are retired.**

Yes _____   No _____

If we assume no knowledge of the target population's likely response,
then we conclude that before a needs assessment uses this question there
is a 50/50 chance that respondents will choose either a "yes" or "no" response. Let us also assume that a 3% sampling error is appropriate. We
now look at Table 3.2 at the 50/50 percentage column and determine that
a sample size of 1,100 is needed with a sampling error of 3%. On the other
hand, if previous studies from similar cities suggested that about 10% of
elderly would be expected to be interested in gambling and choose the
"yes" option, then our sample size requirement for the same sampling

error would be only 400 by looking at Table 3.2. Typically, in a needs assessment questionnaire we may have knowledge anticipated responses to some questions, but not to others. In such cases, using the 50/50 split is the most conservative and prudent choice for selecting sample sizes.

As Table 3.2 shows, the more variability expected in the responses (hence, in the target population), the greater the sample size required. This makes intuitive sense. The more I am interested in studying people who think the same, the smaller the number of people I need in a study. Conversely, the greater the differences among people in a target population, the more people I need to query to understand this population.

The problem is that needs assessments usually consist of many questions and people may differ in their agreement or disagreement on topics covered in a needs assessment. Complicating this problem further is the occasional need for one needs assessment to say something about the views or needs of different groups of people, whether ethnic groups, gender groups, etc. This type of group analysis requires that each group's sample size requirements be considered separately from the overall sample. That is, in a needs assessment where only 30 participants are African Americans and 400 are non-African American, the accuracy of statistics generated for the non-African American population will be much better than that for African Americans.

That is why it is so important to have a clear sense of the purpose and key questions driving a needs assessment, because they have clear implications for types of group analyses that will be conducted. Subgroup analyses have important bearing on the sampling needs, particularly when accurate quantitative estimates of subgroup attributes are necessary. Bear in mind that the greater the need for quantitative estimates, the greater the requirement to have sufficient numbers of participants in a sample.

Participation Rates and Nonresponse. For any needs assessment, the expected response rate also needs to be considered. Not all people selected for a study actually participate, for reasons such as illness, lack of interest, or relocation. If only 70% of selected respondents actually participate in a needs assessment, the sample may need to be increased by 30% to arrive at the desired sample size.

If the reasons for not participating are diverse and not associated with a subpopulation (e.g., low-income respondents), there is no need to be concerned about nonparticipation rates. However, there should be concern about the representativeness of the sample if nonrespondents tend to represent subgroups, such as those based on ethnicity, gender, and socioeconomic status. Solutions to such problems include oversampling of subgroups and/or weighting the responses of underrepresented groups to compensate for their lower numbers.

Weighting responses is beyond the scope of this book and is covered in such books as de Vaus (1990) and Kalton (1983). If weighting is called for, it is best to consult with experienced researchers. What is important is that the adequacy of sample sizes for needs assessments is best considered before undertaking these studies. The weighting of data after the fact should not be relied on. Rather, it should be used only as a last resort to cope with unforeseen underrepresentation of important subgroups.

Understanding sample size requirements for studies is a very complex statistical issue about which several books have been written. (Cohen's [1988] book on power analysis is widely respected, but is not recommended for those with less than an intermediate level of statistical training.) Because of the level of knowledge required, very large or complex needs assessments are best delegated to experienced researchers and statisticians. Even so, it behooves agencies conducting complex and elaborate needs assessments to acquire a basic understanding of sampling to be informed about their information needs.

The method for selecting a sample and sample size is an important consideration when conducting surveys or any type of study. However, it is not the only concern. Other concerns include developing measurement instruments and planning for nonparticipation rates. Combined, these topics bear directly on diverse needs assessment methods. The following chapters will consider each of these topics.

EXERCISE

SAMPLING METHODS AND SAMPLE SIZES

As with needs assessment methods, different sampling methods can be used to accomplish the same task. Even so, various factors are commonly considered that suggest the use of one sampling method rather than another. These factors include resources (time and funding), access to subjects, the target population, and the focus of the needs assessment.

The following exercise will help you think about the strengths and weaknesses of each sampling method discussed. One vignette is presented below. Using the information in the vignette, explain how you would chose a sampling method to accomplish the purpose of the planned needs assessment. Note that information such as the funding available to conduct the needs assessment is purposely omitted. Consider how funding makes a difference in the selection of the sampling method. Also, consider sample size requirements for each case. Questions to answer and a discussion of possible answers follow the vignettes.

VIGNETTE:
Homeless and Mentally Ill Program

A new program was established by a large East Coast city to meet the needs of the mentally ill homeless. It was felt that there was a growing number of homeless mentally ill people who needed social and mental health services. However, very little was known about them, their numbers and needs. A needs assessment was requested by the mayor's office to find out more about this special, growing population. The following purpose and key questions were established for the needs assessment.

Purpose: To understand better the social, economic, and psychological backgrounds and service needs of homeless mentally ill people in the city.

Key Questions:

1. How big is the problem of homeless mentally ill in the city?
2. What typifies the personal and social backgrounds of homeless mentally ill people?
3. What are their social and psychological service needs?

Sampling Methods to Consider:

Simple Random Sampling Method

Convenience Sampling Methods

Quota Sampling Method

Interval Sampling Method

Judgment Sampling Method

Systematic Sampling Method

Snowball Sampling Method

QUESTIONS:

Could you use each sampling method to accomplish the same purpose of the needs assessment? Explain.

_____

_____

_____

How does funding make a difference in the selection of the sampling method? Explain.

_____

_____

_____

How many participants are required for the needs assessment? Explain.

_____

_____

_____

ANSWERS:

Could you use each sampling method to accomplish the same purpose of the needs assessment? Explain.

No. The homeless mentally ill make up a select group of people. The vignette does not state how much money, if any, is available. This is important information, particularly when number estimates of people are requested (Key Question 1), which on a grandiose level could call for a simple random method of all residents in the city, which is obviously not feasible. Hence, given the fact that the target population is relatively small, a simple random method will not prove very useful.

Homeless people are not easy to identify or contact and often are reluctant to participate in studies. Therefore, a convenience method is called for. The quota, interval, judgment, and systematic sampling methods are not feasible because the population does not congregate in one location, nor are individuals easy to find. The method of choice for Key Questions 2 and 3 is the snowball method wherein initial participants refer researchers to others.

Depending on the funding available, the snowball method can also be used for Key Question 1. That is, this method can help locate as many homeless people as possible who are mentally ill in the city to arrive at the number of homeless mentally ill.

How does funding make a difference in the selection of the sampling method? Explain.

As mentioned earlier, if funds were unlimited, the city could conduct an extensive effort to locate all homeless residents using the snowball method, pay participants to participate in the survey, and have formal social and psychological evaluations conducted on participants using licensed clinical social workers or psychologists. With limited funding, the number of participants will need to be restricted and social and psychological status determinations will largely rely on subjective homeless and mental status definitions.

How many participants are required for the needs assessment? Explain.

First, before beginning a needs assessment, operational definitions need to be determined concerning what constitutes "homeless" and "mentally ill." Without definitions, interviewers will use their own subjective definitions, making the entire sample and results unrepresentative. A sample size of 400 was determined to be appropriate. To arrive at this number, the conventional 5% sampling error rate and conservative 50/50 response split was assumed. Using this assumption and selected sampling error rate, Table 3.1 was used to arrive at the sample size requirement of 400.

Chapter 4

INSTRUMENT DEVELOPMENT

Two weeks had gone by since the Needs Assessment Planning Committee finished planning and developed its purpose and key questions for a needs assessment. The Planning Committee was now meeting again to look over the first draft of the questionnaire that Letisha, the program director and designated head of the effort, had created.

John, the Planning Committee's chairperson, looked shocked and restless. Letisha picked up on his feelings and asked, "John, what's the problem? Did I do something wrong?" John replied, "Letisha, nothing's wrong except this questionnaire. It's 45 pages long! Who will sit down that long to read it, let alone respond to it?"

Putting together a questionnaire, writing the questions for it or other data collection instruments,[1] such as surveys or interviews, are tasks that prove more complicated and technical than thought at first. This chapter provides guidelines and recommended procedures to follow in forming a data collection instrument.

QUALITATIVE VERSUS QUANTITATIVE INSTRUMENTS

After selecting a sampling method and sample size, the researcher or delegated person to conduct a needs assessment is ready to develop the data collection instrument or questionnaire. A decision about whether the data will be qualitative or quantitative must be made.

Qualitative data usually implies the use of open-ended or semistructured questions. Interviews are typically considered a qualitative method. Here are examples of qualitative questions, both open-ended and mixed:

Open-Ended:

What kinds of experiences have you had taking drugs?

Mixed:

What kinds of experiences have you had taking drugs? List drugs you have used, such as marijuana, crack, base cocaine, LSD, glue.

Qualitative questions remove the constraints placed on respondents when answering. Qualitative questions have two particular strengths. First, they can lead to valid responses to questions that researchers would not think of immediately. In asking couples about the type of marriage counseling they need, for example, a significant number of couples may list "budgeting finances" as a counseling need, which researchers may not initially have thought of as marital counseling.

Second, qualitative questions reduce or eliminate the natural tendency of respondents to answer in socially appropriate ways, which is called social desirability. Many respondents consciously or unconsciously respond in ways they feel are in keeping with mainstream opinion. For example, many people will fit themselves within five commonly proposed racial/ethnic group categories of White, Black, Latino, Asian, and American Indian. However, as the Census Bureau is learning, interviews with respondents who are given similar choices reveal significant dissatisfaction with these categories. Interestingly, respondents bow to social desirability and will commonly not complain even when data collection personnel are available to receive feedback.

On the other end of the spectrum are quantitative questions. Researchers utilizing quantitative questions and studies are primarily interested in numbers or quantities that reflect attributes, perceptions, opinions, or characteristics of those in a target population. Hence, quantitative questions and surveys commonly use questions that elicit numerical results. Below is an example of a quantitative question.

Circle the drugs you have used in the past month:

1. Marijuana
2. Crack
3. Base Cocaine
4. LSD
5. Glue
6. Other Drugs
7. Have Not Used Any

This question has fixed-choice responses. Using this question researchers could determine the proportion of respondents in the sample who have used any of the drugs listed in the past month. They can also use this question to indicate the proportion of respondents who have used a combination of the drugs listed.

Sometimes questionnaires used for needs assessments include the use of previously developed assessment tools, such as a commercially available standardized instrument (e.g., established substance abuse measures, family well-being measures, self-esteem scales). The coding and analysis of the responses will determine to a large extent whether a needs assessment is qualitative or quantitative. That is, it is the specific type or need for information that determines whether a needs assessment and its measurement instruments are qualitative or quantitative.

If the results of most questions are represented numerically and the analysis consists of aggregating these numerical representations, the study is likely to be quantitative. On the other hand, if the responses are described by the respondents in their own words, then the study is more than likely qualitative. Some may argue that one form is superior to or more valid than the other, but each can be appropriately used as a needs assessment method. The decision to use one form rather than another (or a combination) depends on (a) information requirements, (b) appropriateness to the study, and (c) availability of respondents.

Information requirements mainly refer to the purpose of the needs assessment. If the need is being mandated by the agency itself, there is more flexibility in the choosing of instruments. However, if external stakeholders such as funders require the assessment, it is important to discuss this issue with them to clarify expectations about what type of information and data they consider acceptable. More and more, funders are requiring quantitative data and methods because to many people numbers or statistics represent fixed quantities of the attribute that is being sought, such as a perceived need for counseling or information.

Moreover, quantitative estimates appear to be more scientific. Yet this impression is not necessarily true. Some needs assessments are more appropriately conducted using qualitative data or information, such as when using interviews. For instance, needs assessments conducted for programs such as youth gang programs are usually better carried out using interview methods. This preference is primarily because of the special nature of respondents and the difficulty in querying such respondents with traditional data collection methods. Imagine, for example, the likelihood of handing a formal questionnaire to a serious delinquent who has a second grade reading level. Even if he understood a self-reported questionnaire, he would more than likely be intimidated by the questionnaire because of its institutional appearance.

Anther reason for using qualitative questions and methods is when so little is known about a particular subpopulation that presuming responses to questions is difficult or unrealistic. Consider the difficulty that a researcher would have developing, let alone implementing, a quantitative questionnaire to be used on elementary aged children of prostitutes for a needs assessment on families involved in prostitution.

Regardless of the type of data collection instrument and method used, the wording of questions is critical to obtaining meaningful, interpretable, valid, and reliable data. Objectivity, clarity, and appropriate response options are major factors affecting the success of a needs assessment.

ITEM DEVELOPMENT

Objectivity. To be a researcher who objectively develops and implements a needs assessment instrument is very difficult, for various reasons. One of the most common is an assumption that the need for services, information, or products is already known. Consciously or unconsciously, agency representatives feel that needs assessments will merely confirm what they know already. A military commander who was in charge of a base family service center once declared that he had no use for a needs assessment, even if the military mandated one. He felt he already knew that spouse and child abuse and neglect were the problems facing military families. Hence, other services would miss the mark. Although existing data revealed a need for other services, by focusing on one or a few particular issues, the commander was ignoring other, equally pressing concerns such as helping families with housing relocation and finance management.

Consider the many ways this military commander could influence the design and outcome of a needs assessment, were he to conduct it himself. The questions would probably focus heavily on abuse issues and exclude other questions. At the study's end, the commander would be able to claim that he had conducted a needs assessment, which would perhaps confirm his beliefs about service needs on the base. Unfortunately, this form of subjective selection of questions and design of needs assessments is common.

The following suggestions can help ensure an objective assessment. One of the most important actions to take to promote objectivity is to include the participation of unaffiliated staff or persons external to the organization. For example, program board members, being familiar with the organization and its objectives, can help provide feedback on the needs assessment plans and data collection instruments. Sometimes board members have research training, which enhances the external feedback.

External agencies and organizations can also refer researchers or other relevant individuals to programs seeking outside review of study plans and instrument development. Another option is to procure formally the services of private research firms or college professors. Private research firms have the advantage of the ready capacity to conduct studies of any scope in a timely manner. The disadvantages of utilizing research firms include cost, which may be beyond the budgets particularly of not-for-profit community-based organizations. Another possibility is that research contractors may be overly eager to agree with program personnel.

An attractive option for programs and organizations is to seek the feedback and involvement of academic researchers from local colleges or universities. Research professors are often eager to assist agencies and to accommodate the budgetary constraints of not-for-profit organizations. Moreover, academic researchers sometimes have research projects that can benefit from information gained from a needs assessment.

There are various ways to locate and contact relevant research faculty. One is to call college departments, such as schools of social work, social welfare, psychology, sociology, and education. Another expedient way of locating relevant departments and faculty is to call deans of relevant academic divisions or schools, including deans of schools of social work (or social welfare), schools of arts and sciences and schools of education. These deans or heads of the schools may be able quickly to provide lists of recommended faculty.

The advantages of seeking a research professor who has experience in conducting needs assessments are usually in terms of cost, expertise and objectivity. As mentioned earlier, college researchers are often as interested in learning from the effort and information gained from needs assessments as they are in earning additional income. Typically, the feedback, advice, and assistance provided by academic researchers leads to a well-thought-out needs assessment.

Still, agencies often do not have funds to pay for or find appropriate private research firms or academic researchers. Hence, it is also common for agencies to conduct their own needs assessments entirely by themselves. In such cases, it is recommended that a needs assessment committee be formed to provide external feedback necessary for good planning and implementation of needs assessments. These needs assessment committees should be made up of both members and nonmembers of the organization. The responsibility for carrying out the needs assessment should not be given to such a committee. Instead, others should be delegated this responsibility. However, it is important that ongoing input from the needs assessment committee be provided to researchers throughout the study.

It is also recommended that such a committee include one or more members of the target community. Constant feedback from members of the community provides valuable insight on the sample selection and the wording of the questions. This inclusion is particularly important when the targeted population includes ethnic and linguistic minorities.

Leading Questions. Leading questions are inquiries likely to generate particular responses. For example, the question, "Why do you think marital therapy services should be offered in your community?" assumes that there is a need for marital counseling and compels the respondent to accept this premise. Another leading question is: "Why do you think the community needs substance abuse services?" As mentioned earlier, it is difficult for writers of questions to be objective, because the subject themes they are trying to explore through questionnaires are sometimes inadvertently but heavily influenced by their expectations or desired responses.

To assure that leading questions are excluded from questionnaires, uninvolved persons, whether from needs assessment committees or others, should review the questions developed. In addition, data collection instruments need to be pretested on a small group of members from the target population. Pretesting the questionnaire involves having a representative group of respondents undertake or respond to an initial draft. More is said about this later.

Clarity. Another common problem is the clarity of the questions. We are all subject to our own style of writing and semantic interpretations of words. Yet often respondents have to guess at what the writers meant in questionnaires. For example, what is this questions asking?

How important is individual support to you?

Such a question is usually met with confusion by respondents. However, because of self-consciousness, respondents will force a meaning onto it. To some the question may mean financial support, to others psychological services, to others having a friend to talk to, and to others believing in oneself. Interestingly, the meaning of such questions is obvious to their originators.

Other unclear questions are immediately "understood" by the respondents, but as in the preceding example, have many meanings. Consider the following question:

Do you often think of yourself as being bad?

To some, this question may seem like a good candidate for a self-esteem scale, but if directed at youth, a respondent may mark "yes," feeling they are cool, when the researcher meant otherwise. As with leading questions, the way to avoid this problem is to pretest and individually interview pretest respondents.

Educational Level. Often researchers have a higher education level than the target population. Therefore, questionnaires are commonly constructed at a reading levels beyond those of the respondents. Questions are therefore liable to be misunderstood or incomprehensible. Consider the following example:

Consider for a moment support services you believe are personally imperative, which is most paramount for you?

First, the question assumes the respondent reads at a high level. As a rule of thumb, questionnaires developed for the general population should not be written beyond the sixth-grade level. Second, phrases and jargon, such as "support services" assume familiarity with terms that are not well understood by the layperson.

Again, the best way to avoid this problem is to have likely respondents provide feedback on the questions. Another way to avoid elevated reading levels in questions is to have instruments reviewed by reading level experts, who are commonly found in schools of education. Another option is to have a sixth-grade teacher check the expected reading comprehension. However, neither of these options should substitute for pretesting the instrument on a small number of members of the target population.

Care should be taken to construct instruments that are also culturally relevant—meaning equally understood by ethnically or linguistically diverse people, if they are in the target population. Experts on relevant ethnic groups should be consulted and asked to review the instrument for cultural relevance and sensitivity. Such feedback on the cultural and linguistic appropriateness of the instrument and procedures is important, because it adds to the validity of the study. Again, even a cultural expert is

no substitute for pretesting on cultural group members likely to participate in the needs assessment.

Response Options. Although every question in a survey may be clear, the
response options may be confusing or misunderstood. Response options
should undergo the same scrutiny as the questions. That is, they should
be checked for being leading, unclear, and incomprehensible and they
should be pretested. It is important to consider the type of information
needed when deciding on response options. Besides providing basic information, the types of response options will determine the type of statistical techniques that can be used to analyze the data.

Response options for needs assessments commonly use one of three
main types of *response scales:* (a) categorical or nominal, (b) ordinal, and
(c) interval. Categorical, also called nominal, response scales assign numbers to response choices, but these numbers are arbitrary; one number has
no more value than another. For example, a question on gender can have
a "1" represent males and a "2" represent females, or vice versa. The
number for either has the sole function of distinguishing males from females. With some exceptions (specific only to dichotomies, and outside
of the concern of this book), the statistical analysis of categorical items is
limited to group identification and frequency distributions.

A popular response scale in surveys and psychological tests is the ordinal scale. As with categorical scales, responses are assigned numbers.
However, the ranking of the numbers has additional meaning. An example of an ordinal scale is a five-point agreement/disagreement scale called
a *Likert Scale.* Following is an example of a question using this type of
response scale:

I would definitely use tutoring services if offered.

(1)	(2)	(3)	(4)	(5)
Strongly Agree	Agree	Not Sure	Disagree	Strongly Disagree

Likert scales come in different types. This response scale focused on
level of "agreement." Other scales focus on other characteristics, such as
"liking" (Like Very Much to Not Like at All), and "need" (Need Very
Much to Not Needed at All).

Social scientists make the assumption that the distances between con-
tiguous options of these ordinal scales are equal, which is really a prop-
erty of interval response scales. A question on age is an example of an
interval level question, because the difference between any two contigu-

ous ages is the same throughout the range of ages. However, in social science research there are few instances of true interval level scales. Instead, questions with ordinal properties are more common. The following question serves as an example of an ordinal question:

To what extent do you have a problem with childcare?

1	2	3	4	5
Great Problem	Somewhat a Problem	Not Sure	Somewhat Not a Problem	Definitely No Problem

The difference between 1 and 2, 2 and 3, 4 and 5 or any other differences between response points cannot be considered equal. That is, we cannot say that the difference between persons indicating "somewhat" of a problem and a "great problem" are as equally different as the comparison between those indicating "somewhat not" or "definitely no problem."

However, some argue that the differences are similar enough to assume the statistical properties of normally distributed responses in a sample and a homogeneous variance. In fact, statistical studies have largely borne these assumptions out (see Baker, Hardyck & Petrinovich, 1966). Accepting these assumptions, researchers commonly apply what are called "parametric" or "inferential" statistics to data gained from ordinal questions. Inferential statistics include such statistical analyses as correlations, multiple regression, factor analysis, analysis of variance, etc., all of which are beyond the scope of this book. However, these can and often should be used in needs assessments if experienced researchers are involved.

Many of these sophisticated statistical techniques are used to test or examine the relationships or differences among groups or subpopulations or their characteristics. For example, correlation coefficients are numbers derived through statistical formulas that say something about the strength of a relationship between two variables. For instance, a community needs assessment may reveal a close correlation between community violence and high-school dropout rates. Correlation coefficients range in value from 0 to 1 or 0 to −1. The larger the correlation coefficient the closer the relationship between two variables. Let us say researchers found a .6 correlation between community violence and dropout rates. This statistic would indicate that there is not a one-to-one relationship between community violence and dropout rates, but there is a strong relationship. Researchers would usually be satisfied with a correlation of .3 or greater given a moderate sized sample. More will be said about statistics in Chapter 5.

In general, response options given to respondents will determine the level of analyses possible. Constructing questions that provide response scales at the ordinal level or interval levels of measurement allow the application of inferential or parametric statistics. Nominal response questions can also be analyzed, but are limited to mainly descriptive statistics such as categorical counts or percentages. More will be said about analyses in Chapter 5.

Open-Ended Questions. Issues such as objectivity, leading questions, clarity, and educational level apply to open-ended questions as well. However, with open-ended questions the response is not constrained and the respondent is left to answer freely. This freedom can pose a challenge to those conducting the needs assessment when reporting the results. Options for handling open-ended responses range from reporting selected responses by some participants to make a researcher's point, to categorizing responses and assigning them numerical representation. For example, responses to the question: "Who do you seek help from when you are depressed?" can be placed in such categories as clergy, relatives, friends, or others. Moreover, numbers can be assigned to these categories and frequencies can then be generated to show aggregated responses.

Categorizing open-ended questions is very time consuming and often arbitrary. Problems such as understanding responses, creating too many or too few categories, and spending too much time with them are all issues that concern those who have not planned their coding or analysis and ultimate use. On the other hand, responses given to open-ended questions can be a powerful means of conveying information. Unencumbered responses humanize concerns and allow respondents to make statements that truly reflect their opinions and feelings.

Open-ended questions are particularly useful for needs assessments on subjects not previously studied in great depth. They can yield much new and unanticipated data which can lead to subsequent investigations of that population. The use of a structured questionnaire does not preclude the use of some open-ended questions in the instrument. Instruments using a combination of open-ended and structured questions are sometimes called semi-structured questionnaires. Again, the need for information should determine the use of any type of questions.

Demographic Questions. Basic demographic questions must always be included in a needs assessment to clarify the population of interest. Too often, not enough thought goes into the use of demographic information, because the attention of an agency may be locked into the key questions

for assessing needs. It is suggested that demographic questions on at least
the following variables be included:

- Age
- Gender
- Ethnicity/Race (not just race)
- Income
- Education
- Place of Residence (including neighborhood if ascertaining residency in the
  target area/population).

After key questions for the needs assessment have been identified, consideration of the study's demographic breakdown is essential. It must be
done during the planning stages of the study, because the analysis breakdown will influence the number and type of respondents sought.

PRETESTING

As discussed throughout this chapter, one of the most important tasks
in developing an instrument is pretesting. Pretesting involves administering a draft of the instrument to a small group from the target population.
Although this small group of respondents need not be randomly selected,
consideration should be given to ensuring that a pretest sample reflects
the same social and cultural diversity of the target population. For example, a needs assessment may be planned in a culturally diverse community
where 30% are African American, 30% Latino, 30% Asian, and 10%
White Anglo. It may be the case that more of the White Anglo population
are conveniently accessible through a local Boy Scout troop. However,
pretesting with this subpopulation will negate the feedback given by the
larger Asian, Latino, and African American populations. This would be a
particularly wrong decision to make given the linguistic differences associated with such groups in the community.

Including heterogeneous subgroups is important, because they may interpret the questions differently because of social and cultural differences
or varying reading levels, among other differences. Data collected from
pretesting should never be included in the formal study, because pretest
participants are treated differently, which can lead to biased responses.

During pretesting, respondents are asked about each question to see if
they understood its meaning and whether the response choices were adequate. Regardless of the type of questions used—structured, fixed-choice,

or open-ended—pretest respondents should be interviewed and asked about each question, the response choices used, and instructions for responding to make sure questions and procedures are clearly understood. Pretesting should not be carried out until careful reviews of the instruments and procedures have been done by others, such as by a needs assessment planning committee. Such reviewers should include researchers, community residents (representing the type of respondent used) and perhaps agency representatives from other organizations working in the target area (because they should also be familiar with the population). This review process will help eliminate many obvious shortcomings of the data collection instrument and procedures before undertaking the study. Pretesting done as part of the needs assessment should be documented in any of the papers reporting the outcome.

CONCLUSION

Writing questions for data collection instruments may seem easy, but it is decidedly not. Decisions need to be made regarding their qualitative or quantitative nature and the requirements of the needs assessment. Moreover, particular care needs to be given to possibly confusing factors such as subjectivity, leading questions, assumed educational or reading levels, or inadvertently confusing questions. These concerns also apply to the development of response options given to respondents. Beyond clarity, response options bear on the type of statistics that can be applied to the results, therefore, on the type of information possible to obtain.

It is instructive to return to the purpose and key questions formed after constructing a questionnaire or data collection instrument to make sure that key questions will be addressed by the questions and response choices. Each question should be tied to key questions and the overall purpose of the needs assessment. If not, two options are possible.

The first option is to eliminate interesting but nonessential questions from the study. It is tempting to keep some nonessential questions because they seem important and interesting. However, the longer the questionnaire, the more the time necessary for aggregating, coding, and reporting the results. And time is always in short supply when doing needs assessments.

A second choice is to expand the number or scope of key questions. Sometimes important and relevant areas of inquiry are revealed when questionnaires are written. These discoveries also reveal better areas of inquiry that can substitute for previously planned areas. For example, a community dental health center may have planned to ask about the community's liking of the health center, but later decides that it would be better to assess intended use of the clinic. Intended use of the clinic was the main concern all along, however; somehow "liking" became a substitute for the intended information sought.

Just because many funders and evaluators like to see numbers or quantities resulting from needs assessments does not devalue the importance of open-ended questions. Sometimes the quoted words of a six-year-old who expresses confusion about the crippling effect of severe depression in a parent speaks louder than a number or statistic. In fact, it is highly recommended that even quantitatively focused needs assessments make provisions for collecting qualitative or interview information so that it may be used to highlight quantitative results. The power of presenting a combination of quantitative and qualitative methods in reports should never be underestimated.

As this chapter mentions, successful needs assessments plan to pretest their data collection instruments on a small group of respondents who reflect the social, gender, and cultural characteristics of the target population. Querying the pretest sample on each question and response option is essential. However, it is important first to establish rapport with the pretest sample before administering a questionnaire. Otherwise, respondents will feel uncomfortable and may respond "yes" to every question the interviewer asks.

One final piece of advice for those interviewing respondents using structured or fixed-choice questions: If structured questions are being read to respondents and their answers are noted by the interviewer, placards with response choices should be prepared and used for noting respondents. That is, placards with response choices are shown to respondents, the question is read to them, and respondents then are asked to say and point to the response they select. Using response placards helps respondents see clearly the response options available to indicate their response choice. Respondents are often self-conscious about their participation; placards minimize the need to focus on small-print material or listen to interviewers read response choices. Some researchers create placards for individual responses and hand a stack of these response options to respondents to show or return response options or to read out the number corresponding to that choice. This method of responding is sometimes used with sensitive questions, such as questions on participation in illegal behavior (e.g., drug use or crime) or sexual or personal behavior.

Proper planning and pretesting will save a significant amount of time and make the reporting of the data much easier. In fact, many researchers approach the next step in implementing a needs assessment—analyzing the results—with hesitation and, because of lack of knowledge, procrastination. It is hoped that Chapter 5 will demystify it.

EXERCISES

1. Write a quantitative and a qualitative question on the need for a mentoring program for adolescents (directed at adolescents, not adults or parents). Make sure response choices are written for the quantitative question.
2. After completing items or questions for Exercise 1, pretend you are a respondent. Say something about the success of the writer in writing questions that are:
   - Objective versus subjective
   - Leading questions
   - Clear in meaning
   - Written for the appropriate educational and reading level
   - Clear and appropriate response options
3. Repeat the instructions for Exercises 1 and 2, but use a subject matter that is relevant to you.

NOTE

1. The word "instrument" refers to data collection tools, such as questionnaires or a collection of questions measuring a particular attribute such as self-esteem.

Chapter 5

COLLECTING DATA
FROM PARTICIPANTS

Freda and Bob were charged with interviewing pregnant teenage mothers on the west side of Kansas City. They were told that many of the subjects attended an alternative high school. They only needed 25 for a needs assessment promised to United Way. They went during lunchtime so as not to disrupt classes. When they arrived at the school a tall, heavyset man met them. They explained what they were trying to accomplish. The man turned out to be the principal, Mr. Mendoza, who told them that they needed school district approval. The district office referred them back to the principal, who referred them to a certain person at the district office, who referred them to the state's department of education. Weeks went by without entry into the school.

It is one thing to have a plan and instruments for conducting a needs assessment and it's another to make all preparations for access to the sample sought. At times access to participants is no problem; at other times it can prove extremely difficult. Having access to participants is a privilege, not a right. Researchers may have the most noble of causes and intentions in their needs assessments, but people have a right to refuse participation.

APPROACHING PARTICIPANTS

Gaining the willingness of people to participate in a needs assessment can be achieved through a direct or indirect contact approach. The direct approach entails contacting prospective participants directly, whether personally or through other means (e.g., direct mailing, radio or television broadcasting, flyers, posters). For example, a teenage pregnancy prevention program may want to conduct a needs assessment focusing on the counseling needs of at-risk young women in a particular high school noted for its high pregnancy rate. Because students live in a relatively small community, researchers may decide to mail an appeal letter inviting students to participate in the study by coming to the program's offices located in the community.

Such a decision would generally require more than just an emotional or subjective appeal. Paying or offering gifts to respondents would likely be required if the appeal is based only on helping the agency or program, even if it is clear the agency's motives are to help others. I will provide guidelines for monetary or gift incentives.

The more common mode for approaching possible participants is the indirect approach, which uses the support, endorsement, or direct involvement of intermediaries. Using the teen pregnancy program example, the school could have supported the data collection effort by allowing agency representatives to pass out flyers on school grounds or could have met with program representatives to give them advice on contacting students *(support)*. The high school principal could also volunteer to write a letter of endorsement, which could be presented to students or parents to validate the importance of the study *(endorsement)*. The school could also volunteer to administer a questionnaire during class and in this way become directly involved. In general, the more that relevant organizations are involved in needs assessment efforts, the easier it is to get participation.

Directly relevant agencies are not the only ones who can help with needs assessments; civic and community leaders also can. Respected celebrities, elected officials, or national figures can also help validate the assessment and facilitate access to participants. Community leaders who are highly respected for their concern and involvement can add to the validity of a study. This is particularly important in ethnic minority communities where many may trust only those whom they respect and are members of their cultural group.

Endorsements by respected persons always benefit those seeking access to study participants. However, careful consideration should be given to the possibility of alienating segments of the target population because of a lack of unanimity in views in populations toward such notable figures. Not all African Americans would, for example, look favorably on a needs assessment endorsed by Louis Farrakhan, a controversial Muslim spokesperson. Plans for endorsement should be discussed with members of the target community beforehand.

An important thing to remember is that people respond affirmatively to pleasant, positive, and respectful personal requests for assistance. In contrast, impersonal, formal, and bureaucratic approaches do not have much persuasive appeal, such as a letter of appeal by an unknown bureaucratic head of a federal agency, relevant as they may be. Charities, politicians, and salespersons all know the critical and decisive impact that personal contact has on people. Those seeking study participants need to consider ways they can make personal appeals for participation. It is preferable to have study participation directly follow personal appeals instead of making appointments, because many people would rather not take time later to participate.

FINDING PARTICIPANTS

Methods of finding participants depend on the type and number of respondents needed as well as the level of representativeness desired of the target population. For instance, crack users are relatively small in number and difficult to identify and contact. Therefore, a researcher would be hard pressed to conduct a citywide survey of randomly selected crack users with sufficient numbers to be able to generalize to all crack users.

Finding participants who are members of specialized and relatively small populations usually calls for convenience methods, as apposed to strict randomized experimental methods. The snowball method (discussed in Chapter 2) is particularly useful for access to small and special subpopulations such as drug addicts, delinquents, criminals, prostitutes, and gang members.

Unless a program has ready access to a desired target population, agencies conducting needs assessments should seek the advice and assistance of organizations and their representatives who routinely work and interact with the desired population. Other ways of identifying potential respondents include using name lists, club rosters, phone books, and other publicly available mailing and name lists.

INCENTIVES TO PARTICIPATE

Incentives to participate in a study typically include a sense of moral responsibility or obligation, money, gifts or goods, or program assistance that benefits the respondent. Community-based organizations often rely on a sense of moral obligation or responsibility as an appeal to potential respondents, for two reasons. First, community organizations often have limited funds, if any, to pay participants. Second, many assume that their appeals for participation somehow touch an inherent sense of responsibility and obligation. Sometimes this assumption is borne out, but often it is a false illusion. The effectiveness of moral appeals depends on the centrality of the issue to the target population, the effort and time required to participate, and the sensitive or invasive nature of the topic or topics of the study.

Moral appeals usually lead to participation when opportunities for participation immediately follow appeals. Appealing, then setting up a future appointment, does not lead to the same level of participation because daily life demands compete for a likely respondent's attention.

Survey research has clearly demonstrated the effect that monetary and tangible gifts have on participation rate. It is always recommended to use such incentives if funds permit. Monetary incentives used for research studies vary from nominal amounts, such as one dollar, to those in the hundreds, primarily for medical research.

Barring budgetary constraints, the recommended amounts of incentives for needs assessments depend on the number of participants sought, the amount of time needed to participate, and the personal nature of the topics covered. It is not uncommon for surveys on sexual practices to pay $20 or $30 to gain participation. Focus groups or long interviews can also call for such incentives because of the time commitment required. Targeting a small sample makes it easier or more realistic to pay a higher incentive fee. Apart from focus groups, the average needs assessment takes between 30 to 45 minutes for respondents to complete. With this time commitment in mind, when monetary incentives are used, they range from $10 to $20. Some organizations with fewer funds available will combine a modest monetary incentive with a moral appeal.

Another incentive for participation is the perception or reality that participation will directly or indirectly benefit the respondent, family, or community. In assessments or surveys, schools, for example, will often inform parents that their participation or their children's participation in a study will benefit them, their children, or education's cause in some way. The success of such approaches depends on how clear the link is between participation and purported benefits as well as the sense of obligation to participate that is felt.

MEETING WITH RESPONDENTS: PROCEDURES

I earlier discussed different ways of validating the importance of needs assessments. This section discusses the importance of following standard study requirements and recommended research procedures before securing the participation of respondents. Several requirements or recommended procedures will be discussed in this section:

1. Build rapport
2. Secure written consent
3. Provide basic information about the purpose of the study and type of information required, including the personal nature of the information sought
4. Inform about the voluntary nature of study
5. Reveal possible risks
6. Name the person or office to contact to complain or convey concerns
7. Inform about the type of assurance and protection of anonymity, confidentiality, and possible legal prosecution

Establishing Rapport. One of the first and most important steps to take when meeting with possible respondents is to build rapport with them. Building rapport with likely respondents means helping them feel at ease or comfortable with you. This step is important, because a respondent's attention and comprehension of questions asked through interview or survey, for example, will depend on the level of comfort, anxiety, and trust respondents have with the data collection staff.

To increase rapport at the first meeting, researchers should avoid holding forms, papers, notebooks, writing instruments, or other formal material in their hands. Second, researchers should start introductions with small talk. Reveal some of your background, such as where you are from, and things about yourself that show concern or interest in people and their communities. This rapport building should take 5 to 10 minutes depending on the sensitive nature of the needs assessment and the similarity between participant candidate and interviewer. Securing responses from participants should not take place until rapport is established. Otherwise, responses may be invalid or incomplete.

Consent Form. After establishing trust and rapport, data collection staff will present participants with two copies of a written consent form that contains information about items 3 through 7 above. This consent form is usually read to the respondent, which is followed by asking them if the information presented is clear and if they have any questions. A discussion ensues about what information is contained in the consent form and other information to discuss with participants before they participate. Respondents are asked to sign both copies of the consent form after researchers answer any questions or address any concerns. One copy is kept by the researcher and the other is given to the respondent.

Purpose of the Study. One of the first pieces of information to give respondents about a needs assessment concerns its purpose. Various questions need to be addressed, such as who the researcher is representing and what organization is responsible for the needs assessment. Why is a needs assessment being conducted? What information is being sought? Who will benefit from the results? What incentives are there for participation? How long will participation take? Consider the following portion of a consent form written for a needs assessment of Navy service members that addresses many of these questions:

> Dear Service Member:
>
> Over the past several years, the Navy has been trying to improve the quality of life of its members and their dependents by establishing or strengthening support services, such as Family Service Centers, at Navy commands worldwide. You have been randomly selected to participate in a survey that will greatly assist the Navy in determining current needs and concerns as well as how much people know about existing services. If you participate, you should know that any information you provide will greatly assist those of us in the Navy who make policy and provide services. Some of the questions on family relationships may be personal, but no one will see your responses except the researchers. Participation will take about 30 minutes.

Such information should not only be written into the consent form, but discussed with the participant as well. Knowing the purpose of the study will often also help the respondent understand the context of the questions asked and clarify their meaning.

Voluntary Nature of Study. It is important to make it clear to respondents that participation is totally voluntary. This is particularly important for organizations that have some type of decision-making authority over participants, such as law enforcement agencies, courts, schools, and some federal agencies (IRS, FBI, etc.). It is also important to inform participants that they can stop participating at any time. Consider the following example:

> Participation in this study is totally voluntary. You can stop your participation at any time. You can also choose to not answer any question that makes you feel uncomfortable.

Possible Risks. Participants need to know if they face any physical, psychological, or legal risks by participating. Consider the following statements:

You run no known physical risks if you to choose to participate. However, we do need to tell you that your answers to some of the questions on past involvement in any illegal activities can lead to your prosecution in a court of law if they are incriminating and if this information were somehow revealed to law enforcement personnel. However, this situation is extremely unlikely, because your name will not appear on the questionnaire you complete. Besides, we are interested not in looking at the answers of any one participant, but rather in group responses.

This statement makes it clear that questions on illegal activities will be asked (e.g., use of illegal drugs, participation in crimes), but it also provides assurance to respondents that their answers will be kept confidential. Researchers need carefully to consider all possible risks to participants, to convey these risks to them, and if appropriate, assure them of steps taken to minimize such risks.

Where Participants Can Complain. Respondents need to know to whom they could go or what office they can contact to complain of any improper procedures or information gathered. University researchers have institutional oversight committees called institutional review boards (IRB) that are responsible for making sure that research efforts do not pose psychological, physical, or legal harm to participants. Consent forms normally list the name and phone number of the chairperson of the designated institutional review board.

IRBs can also review and approve plans, procedures, and consent forms to be used by organizations external to the college or university as a public service or obligation. Most large hospitals also have IRBs, which could likewise be used to review and approve research plans and consent forms for external organizations. Feedback from IRBs is almost always important and helpful for revealing unanticipated consequences of studies, which can reduce legal liabilities resulting from improper research procedures.

Anonymity and Confidentiality. Potential respondents need to know whether they will be assured of anonymity and/or confidentiality. There is a difference between them. Anonymity refers to procedures taken by researchers to strip personal identification from responses. Hospitals and health clinics are legally bound to conduct AIDS and HIV tests that assure anonymity. Health facilities take steps to ensure that these test results are not linked to names or personal identifiers.

Confidentiality, on the other hand, refers to efforts that the researchers take to ensure that information about participants is not revealed to others outside of the research staff. Confidentiality procedures include keeping response forms locked up, separating response sheets from names of participants, and promising respondents not to reveal their participation to anyone outside of the research staff.

Risks of disclosure are greatest with confidentiality, but procedures used for anonymity minimize the risk of exposure. Assurances of confidentiality do not necessarily imply anonymity. However, those assuring respondents of anonymity should also take steps to ensure confidentiality. Decisions to assure anonymity or confidentiality should be made clear to respondents and be included in the consent form.

Certificates of Confidentiality. Certificates of confidentiality are legally binding, written assurances by the Department of Health and Human Services that researchers and study participants cannot be subpoenaed in any court of law or asked by law enforcement officials to reveal the identities or information provided by respondents even if the information is incriminating. These certificates are particularly important to obtain when conducting studies asking about respondents' participation in illegal activities (e.g., illegal drug use).

EXERCISES

A community health clinic is beginning an AIDS and HIV program, which will offer HIV/AIDS testing as well as information about behaviors or practices that place people at risk of contracting the HIV infection. A needs assessment was planned with the following purpose and key questions:

Purpose: To assess the community's need for HIV/AIDS testing and related information.

Key Questions:

1. How interested is the community in having HIV/AIDS testing available locally?
2. How likely are members of the community to be tested for HIV/AIDS?
3. How knowledgeable is the community about AIDS and ways of contracting HIV?
4. How interested is the community in being provided with information about AIDS/HIV infection?

Exercises:

1. Using the preceding information, how would you recommend that the health clinic seek access to 50 participants in a needs assessment? Is a direct or indirect approach warranted in making contact with potential respondents?
2. Indicate what type of incentive these researchers need to offer respondents.
3. If the needs assessment chosen was the interview method, list the steps to take before making contact with the participant.
4. Write a consent form for the health clinic that meets the requirements listed in the section on procedures.
5. What type of assurances of confidentiality or anonymity should this needs assessment provide to respondents?

Chapter 6

DATA PREPARATION
AND STATISTICAL ANALYSES

On Friday the youth violence prevention program staff celebrated the completion of interviews with 160 adolescents in the community as part of a needs assessment. John, the person responsible for undertaking the interviews, grabbed the box with the completed interview forms, walked up to Venessa and said, "Good luck, you'll need it! I'm so glad someone other than me got stuck with this ghastly task. I hate numbers, math, and statistics!" Venessa pretended to be in control but later turned to Mr. Ramirez, the director of the program, and said, "Why did you delegate this responsibility to me? What am I supposed to do with these interviews?"

DATA PREPARATION

At this point many people undertaking needs assessments become nervous, if not frightened, by the seemingly daunting task of analyzing the data. As a result, many stare at the completed questionnaires collecting dust on shelves for fear of not knowing what to do. This chapter will demystify this important part of a needs assessment process. The task has three parts: (a) cleaning the data, (b) coding the data, and (c) analyzing the data. One cannot analyze the data before completing the first two steps.

CLEANING THE DATA

Cleaning the data refers to the steps that clarify responses, eliminate incomplete or invalid information, and take stock of usable responses. Data collection instruments are completed by respondents themselves or by interviewers. In either case, responses to questions need to be clear and legible. Using fixed-choice or structured questions reduces this problem, because responses are normally checked off or circled. Even so, sometimes even such responses are confusing, such as when circles encompass more than one response.

What to Do About Missing Responses. Missing or unclear responses to questions should be either (a) considered missing data, (b) obtained or clarified by talking to the respondent, or (c) substituted by the average, median, or modal response of the entire sample. The latter option is usually only adopted when having missing data would restrict the use of desired statistical analyses (more will be said about this issue in the section on statistical analyses).

Ideally, unclear or missing responses should be brought to the attention of respondents so that they can indicate their answers. However, this option is normally not feasible or possible. Missing data is more often than not ignored, with statistics being derived from all but the missing data. Consider the following question:

How old are you? Years: _____

Let us say that 100 people participated in a needs assessment that asked this question, but 5 refused to give their age. The calculation of the average age for the sample would normally exclude the 5 missing respondents. Instead of having the *sum of available ages for the entire sample divided by 100,* the *age sum* is divided by 95 (age sum/number of valid responses).

The problem with this approach to handling missing responses arises when they exceed 5% for any one question. In any study, there is a "normal" or expected statistical probability that any possible response or typical response will result. If we were to examine reasons for nonresponses among the usual 5%, we would find a plethora of reasons for not responding, including not understanding the question, finding it irrelevant, inadvertently skipping it, being offended by it, feeling it was too personal, and not wanting to respond to it, and so on.

As the percentage of missing responses increases so does the likelihood that one reason dominates others for not responding. Researchers should be concerned with finding more than 10% of missing responses. In such cases, efforts should be made to understand the reasons for not responding before conducting analyses on the remaining valid responses. Otherwise, it may be that only one nonrepresentative group responded to the question (e.g., one gender, ethnic, income, or education group).

CODING RESPONSES

Coding data refers to specific plans or methods for aggregating responses or patterns of responses so that statements can be made about key findings of the study based on the overall sample. Once problems with missing or unclear responses are addressed, researchers need to prepare the data for the types of analyses planned that will allow patterns of responses to be documented. The coding of responses from quantitative surveys or questionnaires is typically easier than coding qualitative responses.

Coding Qualitative Data. The main strength of qualitative data is its ability to examine issues as respondents see them, expressed in their own words, without restrictions in responding. Qualitative responses or results can have a powerful impact on their audience. For example, relaying verbatim the actual experiences of spouse abuse by only one person can have a much more overwhelming impact on readers than results of large-scale surveys, regardless of their startling findings.

On the other hand, qualitative methods are criticized for their subjectivity and lack of representativeness of large subpopulations. Moreover, reduced levels of funding for human service organizations, coupled with the need for greater accountability for funds, have resulted in a reliance on quantitative data. Although qualitative data or responses are frequently reported without reference to numbers or proportions, a greater number of researchers are assigning numerical properties to qualitative data. In general, there are two ways to code qualitative data: the "verbatim" method and the "quasiquantitative interview" method.

The verbatim method subjectively pulls out respondents' statements that address the purpose and key questions of needs assessments. The following excerpt from Moore's (1991) book on gangs uses the verbatim method to point to the problem of spouse abuse among some families of gang members:

Yeah, that happened—ah, once in a while. Sometimes when things were not going right for him, you know. It didn't happen every week, but it happened at least once a month. Like I say, he never talked too much, so I didn't know when things were right or when things were bad, but that's when he beat up, or tried to beat up on her, and that's when we knew that things weren't going right for him, you know. [What did you do during those times?] Well, as a youngster, I couldn't do too much, because my dad was a big man. [So you just waited out of the house?] Well, we had to sleep outside of the house, and you know, stay away from him as much as possible. (p. 91)

Coding data using the verbatim method involves looking through interview responses for information on the topic of interest. For example, a key question may suggest identifying and separating out interview responses on the need for help from external sources with marital problems. In such examples, researchers can go through written interviews and highlight or color code the statements referring to a need for help with marital relationships.

One of the biggest challenges to using the verbatim method is for coders to restrict themselves to highlighting responses that are directly pertinent to the objective of the needs assessment. This, again, is an important reason to develop a purpose statement and key questions guiding the data collection, coding, and reporting efforts. Using the verbatim method does not mean the researcher cannot refer to numerical properties or proportions of respondents and their characteristics or to their responses. The quasiquantitative interview method reports verbatim information, but also gives the reader a sense of the numbers or proportions of respondents with particular past experiences, knowledge, views, beliefs, opinions, attitudes, preferences for services, or patterns of behavior, among other information.

Let us again consider Moore's (1991) work on experiences of spouse abuse among families of gang members to illustrate the use of the quasiquantitative interview method:

Only about half of these men and women said that their parents got along well together. A fairly high proportion—especially in recent cliques—saw their fathers beat their mothers occasionally. (20% of the men and women in their earlier cliques witnessed such battery, as did a third of the men and 40% of the women from recent cliques.) Only a small minority experienced this as a routine feature of their home life. (p. 91)

Here Moore (1991) refers to proportions of respondents living through different tragic experiences in their families. She does so although the method used for her study is largely qualitative and interview based. Unless there are adequate numbers of participants and efforts to draw matched comparison groups, differences among subgroups cannot be assigned levels of significance. In the above example, 20% of earlier gang members experienced seeing their mothers beaten, compared to 40% of more recent gang members. Although these differences in proportions may appear significant, we do not know whether they are, in fact, statistically significant. We do not have an objective sense of the significance of these differences. Even so, statements highlighting trends and levels of agreement found among respondents are informative and useful.

Coding Quantitative Data. Quantitative data consist of responses from participants that can be given numerical values. "Seventy-five percent of adolescent females want adult mentors," is a quantitative statement based on questions whose responses were coded numerically. There are various steps in coding quantitative data collection instruments including naming the variables, aggregating the variables by subject area, and assigning numbers to responses.

Most quantitative needs assessments efforts will use statistical computer analysis programs such as SPSS, SAS, BMDP, SYSTAT. Most statistical computer programs require the naming of variables and the assignment of numbers to responses. The following example illustrates this process:

What is your family income? [FAMINCOM]
(Check One)
1. ___ Under $10,000
2. ___ $11,000–$20,000
3. ___ $21,000–$30,000
4. ___ $31,000 or more

Each response was assigned a numerical value and the family income variable was named "FAMINCOM." It could have been named anything. However, statistical programs usually limit to eight the number of characters used in naming variable. Otherwise, we could have named the variable "FAMILYINCOME" (no spaces are permitted in names).

This process of naming variables and numbering responses is undertaken for each question. Next, we identify variables with different subject domains, which are tied to key questions in the needs assessment. For example, five questions may ask respondents about their perceptions of an after-school recreation program in the local community. These perception questions could be composed of such program characteristics as (a) hours of operation, (b) types of recreational equipment available, (c) recreational staff, (d) peers in the program, and (e) organizing neighborhood teams. In this way all questions are tied to specific subject domains covered in a needs assessment.

STATISTICAL ANALYSES

The final section of this chapter introduces the statistical techniques commonly used in needs assessments, which vary in complexity. Two general types of statistical techniques are used: descriptive and inferential.

Descriptive Analyses. Descriptive analyses are the simplest and most commonly used statistical method for reporting needs assessments. Descriptive statistics merely describe the results of a study using the available data and provide little information about the probability that the statistics obtained reflect the "true" statistics if the entire population was surveyed or included in the study. On the other hand, inferential statistics are used to make inferences about the target population. Descriptive statistics include proportions and measures of central tendency and correlation coefficients. Using proportions usually involves reporting the percentage of responses to particular questions. Percentages are frequently used in needs assessments because of their conceptual appeal. That is, it is easy for nonresearchers to understand that 30% of respondents would participate in a local childcare program. Furthermore, percentages are easy to calculate.

One problem with statistical analyses is knowing what to do about missing data. Missing up to 5% of responses to a question is acceptable. Under 6%, the researcher may simply report the percentage of missing data along with the percentage that answered the question excluding nonrespondents. However, if more than 5% fail to respond to an item, selective nonresponding may be suspected. It may signal one of several reasons for nonresponse, including not understanding the question or feeling the question is too sensitive or private. The researcher should be concerned about particular subgroups not responding, which decreases the representativeness of the results.

Measures of Central Tendency. Measures of central tendency are also widely used because of their conceptual appeal. The three most commonly used measures of central tendency are mean, median, and mode. The mean can be used to give the average response for a particular question or item. The mean is calculated by adding the responses of each participant and dividing the sum by the number of participants. Deriving a mean is appropriate when there is little to moderate but even variability in the responses. Using the mean is not appropriate for questions that are nominal or categorical. An example of a nominal question is:

What is your ethnicity:
1. Anglo
2. Latino
3. African American
4. Native American
5. Asian
6. Other

The mean for such a question would give meaningless information. The mean is best used on questions where deriving the average makes intuitive sense, such as for age and where the dispersion of scores is not great.

The median is the middle score in a ranked distribution. For example, a median age of 30 means that 30 is the midpoint score after ranking all ages from the youngest to the oldest. The median is appropriately used with questions that have extremely high or low scores in a distribution. As with the mean, the median is applied to data where the derivation would be meaningful and informative.

The mode is defined as the most frequent score. If we were paid a dollar each time we correctly guessed numbers selected from a hat, and the number 3 was the most frequently occuring number, then the mode would be the best choice. However, in research the mode is seldom reported, because it has limited utility.

Correlation Coefficients. Correlation coefficients, also called "Pearson product-moment correlation coefficients," range from -1 to 1 and are used to show the relationship between two variables. For example, a researcher may want to know if income and education are related. That is, do increases in education and increases in income go hand in hand? If a researcher found .8 to be the correlation coefficient for education and income, this result would suggest that in the sample, increases in income were largely associated with increases in education levels. Correlation coefficients do not suggest cause and effect. That is, a correlation coefficient cannot be used to conclude that higher education will lead to higher income. The possibility that those with higher income are more likely to seek education than lower income people also exists. A correlation coefficient cannot be used to support the "cause" of one variable over another.

A correlation coefficient of 0 suggests the variables are not related to each other, but a correlation of 1 suggests a perfect association. A correlation of -1 suggests that two variables are perfectly correlated, but negatively; that is, as the value of one variable increases the other decreases by the same amount. Negatively correlated variables can also be described as being inversely correlated. Because of its complexity, the derivation of a correlation coefficient is best done with a computer program designed to calculate the statistic.

Measures of Dispersion. As we have seen, measures of central tendency sometimes mask the variability of the scores. Measures of dispersion help with this problem. The three most used measures are variance, standard deviation, and range. Variance simply tells us how much variability of the scores or responses there is around the mean. This explanation is intuitive, but the parameter is not. The raw scores are subtracted from the mean, squared, added, and divided by the total number of observations minus one—all part of a statistical formula. The variance is needed to derive the standard deviation, which is a more useful and understandable parameter.

The standard deviation is the square root of the variance. To use the standard deviation, however, we need the mean. Once the mean is derived, a standard deviation of responses to one needs assessment question will tell us that 68% of all responses to the question fall around plus or minus 1 standard deviation around the mean. For example, if the mean response to a question is 5 and the standard deviation is 2, then we know that 68% of all scores fall between 3 and 7 (5 minus 2 and 5 plus 2). SD is the common notation for the standard deviation.

The range is the simplest measure of dispersion to calculate, but also the crudest. It is the distance on the number scale over which the scores vary. In other words, it is the difference between the largest and the smallest number. It can be meaningful when scores are pretty much evenly distributed, but is meaningless when scores are not. The range can be meaningful for the following scores: 1, 3, 5, 7, 9 (range = 9 - 1 or 8), but is less meaningful for these scores: 1, 1, 1, 1, 9 (range = 9 - 1 or 8—the same range as in the previous scores).

Inferential Statistics. As the term suggests, by using inferential statistics, sometimes called sampling statistics, we attempt to use characteristics of a sample to infer those of a population. A statistic derived from a sample can be used as a measure to infer that of the targeted population. The representativeness of a sample (whether randomly selected or not) and its size affect the statistical confidence levels. There are statistical formulas that estimate the amount of error in a sample statistic as compared to the true population statistic (e.g., extent to which a sample mean reflects a population mean).

An in-depth discussion of inferential statistics and statistical formulas that assess probabilities of measurement is beyond the scope of this book. However, most computer statistical programs can generate statistics that indicate the level of confidence that a sample statistic reflects the population statistic. However, most inferential methods are used to compare two or more sample statistics, such as sample means, and to determine whether the differences in these sample statistics are significant beyond chance.

Let us say, for example, that the mean request for individual therapy services was derived for each of two racial groups through a needs assessment and were as follows:

TABLE 6.1 Commonly Used Inferential Statistics in Needs Assessments

Statistic	Common Application
Involving Means:	
Student *t*-test	To test for differences between means. Example of a question to test: Does men's mean response to one item differ from that obtained for women?
Involving Variances:	
X^2 test	Testing for differences between variances. Example of question to test: Is the variability in responses to one question the same between one ethnic group and another?
Involving Frequency Data	
z test	Testing for differences between proportions or percentages. Example of hypothesis to test: The percent of high school graduates using illegal drugs is different from the percent of high school dropouts using illegal drugs.
Involving Correlation Coefficients	
z test	Testing for differences between correlation coefficients. Example of hypothesis to test: The correlation between education and family income is the same for Anglos as it is for Latinos.

$$\overline{X}_{Black} = 18.30,$$

$$\overline{X}_{White} = 13.10$$

Are these differences significant? A *t*-test is performed applying a particular formula using a statistical analysis program. Such a program will provide a "t" number as well as a probability:

$$t = 3.4$$
$$p < .01$$

Without needing to understand the meaning of the "t" value, you can see that a "p" value of less than ".05" is provided (which is less than the conventional minimum probability of .05 for assessing significance). This "p" value tells us that the differences between Blacks and Whites in need of marital therapy (comparison of means) are significant where Blacks indicate a greater need for such services than do Whites.

A complete discussion of inferential statistics is beyond our scope. What is important to keep in mind is that inferential statistics can provide information from a sample about the generality of findings. Examples of commonly used inferential statistics are listed in Table 6.1 and described in detail in Glass and Stanley (1970).

CONCLUSION

This chapter considered the basic transformations of the "raw" responses or data, called coding, needed before analysis. Much planning is needed to decide the qualitative and/or quantitative nature of data sought and its ability to address the purpose and key questions of a needs assessment. The chapter discussed the strengths of qualitative and quantitative data and the ways that both are reported.

The technical nature of quantitative data warrants the involvement of a statistical consultant for those who are inexperienced but convinced of the need to use quantitative data (particularly inferential statistics). Another very important step in successfully conducting a needs assessment is reporting the data.

EXERCISES

An early childhood program was recently funded that promoted parents' early stimulation of their children's mental, physical, and emotional development. A needs assessment was conducted on teenage mothers to assess their interest in the program. The following purpose and key questions were agreed on.

Purpose:
> To assess interest and likely participation among teenage mothers in an early childhood program designed to stimulate their children's mental, physical, and emotional development.

Key Questions:
1. How many teen mothers are interested in such a program?
2. What do mothers say about their attachment to their children?
3. How many mothers have heard of the early childhood program?
4. How do these young mothers describe their relationships with their own mothers?

5. How would teen mothers describe their children's mental, physical, and emotional needs?

Exercises:

1. Indicate what type of data you expect to code based on each key question (quantitative or qualitative [verbatim and/or quasiquantitative interview data]).
2. For each key question, indicate the ways the expected data would be analyzed and, if applicable, the type of statistics possible with each.

Chapter 7

REPORTING THE FINDINGS

"Sasha, I don't understand what else we could have done to convince the government that we need funding for early childhood services. We talked to them about the data from our needs assessment, which showed that parents in our community really need these services. I'm beginning to think that our needs assessment was nothing but a waste of time. We shouldn't have listened to our board!"

Three common errors are made when undertaking needs assessments: (a) not documenting findings, (b) not providing findings in useful formats, and (c) not disseminating findings. Not documenting findings is common because not enough time or resources are allocated to this important phase. Not providing findings in useful formats is common not only to service agencies, but also to researchers who are used to writing to academic audiences in technical and theoretical jargon. What good is conducting needs assessments if the information is kept in desk drawers, collecting mothballs?

Conducting a needs assessment and undertaking appropriate analyses are meaningless if information is not presented in an appropriate manner. As the vignette illustrates, to some people "appropriate" dissemination means simply meeting with relevant stakeholders and verbally explaining to them the highlights of the study's findings. As important as verbal communication is, a well-organized and cogently written document complements oral presentations. It serves as a useful and effective communicator, showing the seriousness of findings and conveying the messages you wish to deliver to stakeholders. The best ways to deliver empirical information, however, require early planning, allocating sufficient time and resources to this important task. The suggestions made in this chapter are by no means exhaustive, but point to common forms of preparing and disseminating information to stakeholders in an organized and practical manner.

WHO NEEDS THE INFORMATION?

Before writing up your findings, ask yourself an important question about who desires the study: Who are the stakeholders—those to whom we wish to convey the findings? Having stakeholders clearly in mind before writing results allows you to consider the type of information that would satisfy each stakeholder. Consider this list of common stakeholders for human service agencies:

- Funders
- Agency board
- Agency/organization administrators—including divisions or departments
- Public or program/agency users

These are common groups of stakeholders who initiate a request for a needs assessment or are eager to use the information gained from it. Usually, one main stakeholder initiates the study, but one must still consider the others who may become interested in the results. Typically, main stakeholders are the funders whose focus is to establish the need for services or programs. They are concerned with whether the findings justify the services. When boards and agency administrators initiate needs assessments, the focus is less on establishing a need and more on ensuring the availability and delivery of services, in contrast to public or user group concerns, which focus more on ensuring access to and effectiveness of services. Any stakeholder can be interested in needs assessments for any or all of these reasons. The point is to understand both who has a vested interest in conducting a needs assessment and what type of information they expect to be derived from one.

Sadly, the majority of needs assessments are undertaken simply to justify the continuation of agencies, programs, or services to funders. This situation is unfortunate because, regardless of stakeholder information needs, data derived from needs assessments can be fruitfully used to help improve existing services and programs and their access to subpopulations in a target area. No matter how successful human service programs are, there is always room for improvement.

The following suggestions maximize the benefits derived from needs assessments by setting out a guide for documenting and disseminating empirical findings. Documenting needs assessments in written form is important for fully considering the relevance of the findings to the service agency and its benefactors.

This chapter describes a single report format useful to a variety of stakeholders, ranging from those who want simple and summarized information to those wanting a fuller presentation of the findings. The report format is made up of the following sections: (a) Executive Summary, (b) Introduction, (c) Method or Procedures, (d) Results, (e) Discussion or Conclusion, (f) Recommendations, (g) References and Bibliography, (h) Appendices.

EXECUTIVE SUMMARY

The summary is the most important part of any report, whether called executive summary, summary, abstract, or anything else. You need a short summary of the report that highlights the findings of the needs assessment. Increasingly, executive summaries are being required by stakeholders in documents reporting the results of needs assessments. An executive summary allows readers to become quickly familiar with the major findings, conclusions, and recommendations of the study.

One popular style presents brief summaries of each section in the full report (i.e., introduction, method/procedure, results, discussion/ conclusion, and recommendations). The advantage of this format is that it is easy to read and to find the information from sections that are of particular interest. For some, the interest is only in the results or recommendations, and for others, the methods section is critical for assessing the validity of the findings. This format allows these two groups to be satisfied. It also ensures at least minimal descriptions of each section, including the methodological section, which describes the procedures used to conduct the needs assessment. One could use subtitles for each report section summarized, or the information could simply flow without them, following the same sequence used in the fuller report.

Only significant and important findings should be included in the executive summary. Important findings are those addressing the key questions of the needs assessment. This summary is an effective tool for marketing human service organizations or agencies and for drawing attention to the needs identified by the study.

Executive summaries are almost always attached to the main report, but can also be bound separately. In this way, they prove an economical means of disseminating key information without having to send the full report. This option is important for agencies with limited budgets but large distribution lists.

An alternative to the formal executive summary is a simple summary or abstract of the report. These summaries are usually between 300 to 1,000 words long. As with the executive summary, information from each report section is included, but here very briefly. The advantage of this format is its appeal to busy stakeholders who want to become aware of the needs assessment and its findings without trudging through a mountain of pages. The disadvantage is that only a limited amount of information can be included, making very comprehensive or complex needs assessments difficult to report.

An executive summary in no way substitutes for a full report. A full report is important for both human service agencies and their constituents. It allows for a complete presentation of the study and its findings. Besides documenting the study in greater detail, a formal report serves as a guide for undertaking future needs assessments. The following discussion on each part of a needs assessment report is important to consider when writing an executive summary, which is typically compiled from them.

INTRODUCTION SECTION

The first section of the main report is the introduction. This section presents the general reason for a needs assessment along with the pertinent background information about the target community and population. Essentially, here the reader should become informed about the agency on whose behalf the needs assessment is being conducted and the target community and its relevant characteristics, and become convinced of the need for the information emerging from the needs assessment.

Information about other relevant studies and their findings is appropriate to mention in this section. Commonly included is a formal background that provides essential information about the nature of the social problem(s) in question (e.g., substance use, violence), the community, the agency/organization in question and the services being offered, and any known or suspected needs. The introduction should always end with a statement about the purpose of the needs assessment. The end of an introduction can look like this:

> The answer to the following questions may help us understand the need for spouse abuse services in the Twin Oaks Apartments:

This statement should be followed by a list of key questions of particular interest in the study. Alternatively, hypotheses can follow a purpose statement. For example, an agency may include, among other hypotheses, one suggesting that women with a college education may be less likely to need services than those with less education. It is important that the methodology addresses the key issues or hypotheses mentioned at the end of the introduction.

METHOD SECTION (PROCEDURES)

The method section is typically divided into four subsections: (a) subjects, (b) instruments, (c) procedures, and (d) statistical analysis. Each topic can be titled as a subsection or it can be addressed without subtitles.

Subjects. The first subsection should clarify the description of the subjects. Such information includes the number of subjects recruited, the method of recruiting (mentioning incentives or services provided), the number of attritions and their reasons for not participating, incentives given to participate, and the information given to participants about participation and the nature of the study (including an informed consent form and information about potential risks). All of these topics need to be briefly and cogently discussed. A clear description of the target population and geographic boundaries are also here presented.

Instruments. A description of the data collection instrument is included in the instrument section. Often the entire data collection instrument is included in the report's appendix for reference. This subsection provides a justification for the use of the type of instrument and describes how the instrument was designed and by whom. It is important to mention any standardized or previously used scales or questions included in the instrument. It is often helpful both to describe the types of questions asked (open-ended, structured, etc.) and to include a few representative examples.

Procedures. This subsection offers a general description of the methods used to collect the data. Sometimes only a procedure section is written, excluding a more general method section, because the procedure section reveals how the study was conducted. For example, if interviews were conducted, this section would concisely describe how the respondents were approached, how long the researchers were in contact with subjects, and follow-up plans. The procedure section provides enough information about how the data were collected so that anyone would be able to replicate the study using the information provided.

Statistical Analysis. The method section should briefly discuss the type of analysis planned and the methods used. For example, a report can state something as simple as "The frequency distributions for each item in the questionnaire were generated using the Statistical Package for the Social Sciences (SPSS), version X." The specific statistical analyses should be mentioned for testing any hypothesis proposed in the introduction. If the study is qualitative, there is no need to mention statistical analyses, but the writer should state how the results will be reported (as case studies, for example).

It is vital to consider the type of statistical analyses to use before collecting data. Often, by planning the statistical analysis beforehand, the researcher can see whether the types of questions used and their response choices will lead to the results sought. The researcher often gets caught up in the mechanics of developing questions and putting the questionnaire together, forgetting to ensure that the items developed will generate relevant information. Once the data is collected, the questions and their associated response choices will dictate the type of information available to answer the key questions of the study.

RESULTS SECTION

The results of the study are explained in the results section, which can be difficult to write if more analyses were conducted than originally planned. The problem comes when those conducting a needs assessment get lost in the abundance of collected data and the many seemingly important new questions that the data address. As tempting as new issues may be, it is important to focus on the original purpose of the study, to maintain direction and purpose.

The questions thought important at the start of the study should be used as guides for reporting the results of the needs assessment. This procedure does not preclude addressing other questions beyond those originally conceived. However, they should be clearly identified as additional questions. Questions pertinent to the study should be grouped by subject matter, to make them easier to report and read. For example, information from demographic questions can be reported in a subsection, "Sample Profile" or "Sample Description." The first set of results to report should be those that describe the sample demographically. This information will be used to determine the sample's representativeness of the target population.

It is important for the writer to avoid interpretation of the findings in the results section. Speculations about the reasons for certain results should be left to the discussion section. The writer should simply report the findings as objectively as possible.

DISCUSSION SECTION

The discussion section allows the writer the liberty to take meaning from the results of the study. This section begins by reminding the reader about the purpose of the study, then alerts the reader to any weaknesses or limitations of the study that may have been responsible for the findings, and allows the writer to make general statements about the findings of the study.

The discussion section should begin by reminding the reader of the importance of and need for the needs assessment in a few summary statements. This reminder is commonly followed by a discussion of the weaknesses of the study that could have influenced the results of the study (although researchers sometimes leave this for the end of the section). An example of a possible bias in a study is the use of a convenience sample. This is particularly important to mention if the sample was distinct in some way (e.g., comprised mainly of women). The listing of potential biases should be followed by the writer's view on the likelihood that the biases were responsible for the results.

Following a discussion of the strengths and weaknesses of the data is a summary of the most important and salient findings related to the key questions guiding the study. This should not restate the result section, but highlight the dominant findings, including a discussion of their meaning. This is an appropriate time to mention any subjective and educative reactions of the researcher to the results. In essence, this section helps the reader understand the overall significance of the findings.

Following the discussion section should come the conclusion. If there is no conclusion section, conclusions to the study need to be made at the end of the discussion section. The end of any report should include a wrap-up discussion, which helps the reader understand the bottom line about the study findings. What did the study say about the needs of interest to the organization or agency? Was there evidence of a need for information, products, or services?

CONCLUSION AND RECOMMENDATION SECTIONS

As mentioned earlier, conclusion sections are optional; however, presenting conclusions in some way needs to be a part of any report. The conclusion helps the reader make sense of the study and its findings. Another optional section, which could be incorporated into the discussion section or conclusion or be the final independent section of the report, is the recommendation section. Recommendations translate the findings and conclusions into decision making and positive change. Recommendations help those in decision-making positions (e.g., agency/organization directors or policymakers) to make informed decisions based on empirical data.

Recommendations can mention the need to conduct ongoing needs assessments as well as the need for funds for services or policy changes. The recommendation section is another form of the bottom line for the study. It addresses the question, "What should be done with the information generated?"

This book omits a discussion section because discussions about the topics presented were included in each chapter. The omission of a discussion section allowed leading directly into a conclusion section.

REFERENCES AND APPENDICES

References or recommended reading material come next, followed by the appendices. Some agencies or organizations prefer to have a thin report, so they rely on the appendix sections to contain detailed information that may not be included in an internal report. This section could include large portions of the method section as well as a detailed explanation of the statistical analyses conducted. The data collection instrument can also be appropriately placed in an appendix section. Finally, copies of newspaper articles or other relevant printed information can be included in the appendix. A table of contents is recommended to help the reader find the sections of the report, including the contents of the appendices.

EXERCISES

Philip is the director of a youth diversion program, which is part of an independent, not-for-profit, community-based program. Several changes of the program have been informally recommended by the youth who come to the program. Teachers in local schools have been asking Philip to focus on conflict resolution skills through sports activities. Equal proportions of the program's funds come from the YMCA, the city, annual community fundraisers and the Department of Justice. Public criticism of night basketball and other diversion programs, plus increased competition for funding, have led Philip to conduct a needs assessment.

1. What are possible reasons for Philip's interest in a needs assessment?
2. Who are all the stakeholders?
3. Rank the stakeholders in order of importance.
4. Briefly state what type of information goes in each of the report sections listed below.

5. Put these report sections in their appropriate order without referring to the chapter.

Order (number)   *Information Contained*

_____ Method or Procedures

_____ Discussion or Conclusion

_____ Recommendations

_____ Introduction

_____ References and Bibliography

_____ Executive Summary

_____ Appendices

_____ Results

Chapter 8

SOCIAL AND CULTURAL CONSIDERATIONS

"Joe, these numbers are interesting, but with only 20% of the local population indicating they need our services, I can't see how we can justify the program to our funders." Mary, the executive director, left for her office, called Dr. Margarita Rodriguez, a local university researcher, and contracted her to help make better sense of the data.

A few weeks later, Dr. Rodriquez began her presentation on the results by saying, "Your findings are incredible! I have never seen so much documented need for your type of services anywhere! More than 95% of your Latino and African American populations indicate dire need for your services. Particularly important is the 93% of single mothers who are clamoring for your help. With these data you can leverage your funding from several sources."

Mary and Joe, their mouths agape, stared at each other with puzzled looks on their faces.

As this vignette suggests, sometimes when averaging the findings from needs assessments, researchers overlook the needs of important sub-populations in the catchment area. The world is becoming increasingly complex as diverse populations interact more with one another. Increased population mobility, communications, and international commerce are among prominent reasons why those in human service fields need to develop more competence in understanding diverse populations.

Demographics indicate that the United States's population is more culturally diverse than ever. The 1990 census shows, for instance, that two out of five residents in California are ethnic minorities (i.e., Latinos, African Americans, Asians, or Native Americans). However, cultural diversity is only one of several ways that populations differ. Women are becoming increasingly involved in social and economic areas previously dominated by males. They are increasingly represented in corporate boards, legislative bodies, and the white-collar workforce. Similarly, as an aging society, the United States will need to accommodate an increasingly older population. Human service fields will need to design their programs to accommodate this growing social and cultural diversity.

In no area is this need to be sensitive to diverse populations more important than when conducting data collection, as in undertaking needs assessments. Although this point may seem intuitive, too many empirical assessments are undertaken with little consideration for the diversity in a catchment area. This chapter points out subject areas in need of consideration when undertaking research efforts involving diverse populations. These considerations include language, culture, gender, investigator characteristics, and other social variables associated with the target population. Recommendations are offered at the end of the chapter for developing cultural sensitivity.

FIRST STEP:
KNOW THE TARGET POPULATION

Knowing well those in a target population or catchment area is the first step in assessing the social and cultural diversity in the target area. As discussed in the Introduction, it is critical to define and be clear on the physical boundaries of a target community. After knowing these, secondary data sources such as census data can be easily accessed to determine relevant social and cultural characteristics of the community, such as ethnic and racial group composition, age ranges, educational levels, marital and family status, and other pertinent variables.

LANGUAGE

One cannot emphasize enough the importance of language in conducting effective needs assessments. Concerns around language relate to both oral and written communication. Oral language concerns are most important when using interview methods and written concerns are critical for paper-and-pencil surveys and questionnaires.

WRITTEN LANGUAGE

If there is only one linguistic group in the target area (e.g., English), then only literacy—comprehension, vocabulary, and reading levels—need to be considered. If the population vary significantly in levels of illiteracy, it may be best to select oral data collection methods or to administer written questionnaires orally. As mentioned, most written questionnaires or data collection instruments designed for adolescents or adults are written on no higher than the sixth-grade level. When involving low-income populations, it is best to construct questions at the third-grade level. This level may also be important for populations that have acquired English as their second language.

After settling on a reading level, the issue of comprehension becomes important. To an investigator interested in assessing Spanish-language proficiency, the following question may seem perfectly clear:

How well do you speak Spanish?
   A. I speak it all the time.
   B. I speak it sometimes.
   C. I hardly speak it.
   D. I never speak it.

If the investigator used this item, the responses would be difficult to interpret because what the respondent meant when answering it may not be what the investigator thinks. One might be very fluent in Spanish yet correctly chose any of the responses, depending on *how often* one speaks Spanish. That is, a fluent Spanish speaker may indicate "hardly speak it" because, although fluent, she or he never has occasion to speak it. For this reason questions need to be pretested. Comprehension becomes a particular problem for cultural and linguistic minorities who lack the investigator's vocabulary, preference for words, or local idioms.

Non-English Questionnaires. About one of four residents of the United States does not speak English (Marin & Marin, 1991). This fact poses a challenge to researchers of linguistically diverse subpopulations. On the surface, it may seem a simple task of translating or creating questionnaires in foreign languages. However, the matter is not this simple. Typically, investigators will create instruments in their own language then seek to translate them. But because language has both form and meaning, one must obtain translations that focus primarily on meaning or form. Form-based translations are called literal translations; meaning-based translations are called idiomatic translations (Larson, 1984). Consider the following example translating English into Spanish:

How happy are you?	**[Original]**
¿Que feliz esta usted?	**[Literal Translation]**

Idiomatic or meaning-based translations focus on converting whole questions into equally meaningful questions in another language. The concern is not so much with finding equivalent foreign words for each word, but in using words and phrases to convey the same meaning. Using the previous example, an idiomatic or meaning-based translation could result in the following:

How happy are you?   **[Original]**
¿Que tan feliz se encuentra?   **[Meaning Based]**

Although literal translations are more precise in form, idiomatic translations yield more culturally meaningful translations.

Marin and Marin (1991) mention four common translation techniques: (a) one-way translation, (b) translation by committee, (c) double translation, and (d) decentering. Taking the right precautions, each may be equally valid, but they differ in complexity. One-way translation is the simplest, relying on the judgment of one or more individuals who are well acquainted with the objectives of the study to translate the instruments using either literal or transliteral methods. The problem with one-way translation is that it relies wholly on the knowledge of a select number of individuals. Translations by committee involve having two or more individuals translate the instruments independently, then make decisions about the appropriateness of each. In this evaluation, either the translators come together or a third, impartial person makes final decisions, based on an assessment of the translations.

Double translation takes one-way or committee translations a step further by having another bilingual person translate the interpretation from the foreign language back to the original language. Decentering adds an evaluative step to any of the foregoing methods. This procedure centers around evaluating the cultural relevance and equivalence of both the original wording and its translation. An example from Marin and Marin (1991) shows how decentering works. Consider the following question:

Does your girlfriend share in household duties such as shopping and washing dishes?

In this casual question "girlfriend" in English really refers to a person who is more than a friend. A literal translation of "friend" into Spanish would be "amiga," which fails to connote anything more than friendship. A more appropriate translation, which reflects the meaning of the question would be "novia," which in English is best translated as "girlfriend." In such cases, decentering dictates that changes be made in the English and Spanish wording to make both words more equivalent instead of being centered on the language of origin. In this way the wording is decentered.

Successful translations require not only the appropriate use of the foregoing translation methods, but also cultural knowledge held by those translating. The same words in a particular language can hold different meanings by members of the same ethnic or racial group. After an academic presentation by an American, a British member of an audience passed by the presenter and said, "Your presentation was quite good." The American was instantly elated at what seemed a fairly lofty complement. What he failed to realize was that the Brit was really saying the presentation was barely adequate.

Here is another comical example of incongruent meanings assigned to the same words by members of a particular ethnic group, in this case, Latinos. A Puerto Rican was riding a bus with his Cuban girlfriend and her brothers. The boyfriend excitedly asked for his girlfriend's "pepita," or the pit of the peach that she had just finished eating. Her brothers overheard, and, infuriated, were about to assault him when she intervened, explaining that what he meant was the fruit's seed and not her vagina, as many Cubans understand the word to mean (Soriano, 1993).

These examples show the diversity found in racial or ethnic groups. Effective translations, then, require not only a linguistic command of the language, but also of its use in particular cultural contexts. Those interested in effective translations should ensure that translators are knowledgeable of the relevant cultures.

ORAL LANGUAGE

Many cautions about translating hold true for oral methods as well. An understanding of the culture, its practices, and modes of communicating are critical. For example, among Asian cultures, maintaining direct eye contact—particularly between members of the opposite sex—can be disrespectful. In many Latino cultures, the direct reference "you" or "tu" is inappropriate among new acquaintances. Instead, the more formal "usted," best translated "thou," is more expected. These linguistic nuances can mean the difference between gaining rapport and losing it. What is difficult for researchers to overcome is the fact that respondents often maintain smiles and agreeing gestures even when they feel insulted by the investigator's poor use of words and gestures.

CULTURAL SENSITIVITY

Ideally, all investigators undertaking needs assessments would be culturally sensitive and their decisions and behavior "culturally relevant." Although we have all heard such imperatives, few people understand what is meant by cultural sensitivity or cultural relevance and how to achieve them. Before understanding cultural sensitivity, however, it is important to understand culture and its importance. For our purposes, culture refers to:

> Distinct, preferred (idealized) or performed patterns of behavior (e.g., practices), communication and cognitions that are held in common and accepted by members of a distinct group of people.

Broken into its conceptual parts, this definition suggests that culture has the following components:

Distinct patterns of:

1. Behavior (e.g., shaking hands [Western], bowing [Asian], women avoiding talking to men [some Middle Eastern cultures]).
2. Communication—both verbal and nonverbal (e.g., direct relaying of feelings, emotions, and wishes [Western], avoiding revealing them [Latino, Asian, and other non-Western cultures]).
3. Cognition (attitudes, beliefs, and norms—e.g., women should not be expected to work [non-Western], mental illness as a curse [some indigenous Latino cultures]).

It is the combined patterns of behavior, communication, and cognition that sets one cultural group apart from another. However, some cultural groups may share particular cultural patterns, while not others. For example, most Latino subgroups may hold family-centered cultural values, yet differ on other values. Moreover, there is a difference between clutural preferences or ideals and their actual adoption and practice. For example, some cultural minority groups, such as Latinos, may hold traditional family roles as ideal, but actually practice more egalitarian roles.

The aforementioned definition allows for members of minority groups to be bicultural or multicultural (Harrison et al., 1991; Ramirez & Castaneda, 1974), that is, behave or perform in accordance with the expectations of the dominant culture, although preferring a different and distinct form of behavior (e.g., traditional practices), communication (verbal and/or nonverbal language), and cognition (attitudes, beliefs, values, norms, and roles).

In a seminal paper that reviewed the literature on the importance of culture to cognition, emotion, and motivation, Marcus and Kitayama (1991) pointed out the importance of culture to one's conception of oneself in relationship to others. Two macro conceptions of self, dependent and interdependent, corresponded to Western and non-Western conceptions, respectively. The Western independent conception of self is individually focused, placing great importance on meeting the needs of oneself apart from others. On the other hand, the non-Western interdependent self, manifested in Asian and Latino populations, is embedded within family and others.

Relevance of Culture to Needs Assessments. These findings on the importance of culture have implications for research and conducting needs assessments. They suggest that the task of assessing needs among cultures with origins in non-Western countries requires broadening studies to include the needs of families and socially meaningful others (e.g., social support networks, extended family). Assessing the need for substance abuse treatment services involving Asian populations, for example, may require including questions about the importance of the services to family and friends. Conversely, the same investigation among non-Western independent populations (e.g., Anglos) may more appropriately center on measuring the needs of individuals, separate from families and friends.

A caution should be added to these suggestions, however. It is becoming increasingly important that human service programs and researchers working with cultural groups be careful not to overgeneralize. Latinos are a heterogeneous population. Cuban Americans, for example, are significantly older, more educated, and affluent than Mexican Americans or Puerto Ricans. Furthermore, members of any cultural minority group can differ in their adherence to traditional cultural values and practices. This adherence differs depending on such factors as length of time in the United States, proximity to the country of origin, language usage, and the ethnic composition of the community of residence. *Acculturation* and *assimilation* are important concepts used to discuss cultural change among ethnic minority populations.

Acculturation and Assimilation. Acculturation is defined as "one type of culture change—specifically, change occurring as a result of continuous contact between cultural groups" (Keefe & Padilla, 1987, p. 15). Acculturation is typically used to discuss the adoption or adaptation of ethnic minority groups, such as Native Americans, to dominant Anglo-Saxon cultural values. Although many social scientists have used acculturation and assimilation interchangeably (see Ramirez & Castaneda, 1974), more recently the terms have been differentiated. Assimilation refers to the acceptance and integration of ethnic minorities into society by the dominant culture (Keefe & Padilla, 1987). It is assumed that acculturation is a necessary precondition to assimilation, but not a guarantee of it. In fact, research suggests that the assimilation of ethnic minorities is more the exception than the rule (Keefe & Padilla, 1987).

Conducting needs assessments in culturally diverse populations requires the researcher to be sensitive to the levels of acculturation and assimilation that are likely in the area of focus. Less-acculturated populations are likely to be limited in English proficiency and adhere to the cultural values of their country of origin. Knowing this likelihood may have implications for the language and wording used in the needs assessment instrument.

In the case of Latinos, for example, there is great variability in levels of acculturation and assimilation. It is important to recognize that physical characteristics may be poor indicators of acculturation, because low-acculturated, high-acculturated, or assimilated groups of the same ethnicity may look the same. Those undertaking needs assessments should become familiar with the ethnic or cultural groups in their catchment area before undertaking a needs assessment.

A silly yet unfortunate experience relayed by a Chinese-American colleague from San Francisco serves as an example of the confusion that can be created by false assumptions. An Anglo-Saxon male recently had praised her for "speaking English so well" to which she politely responded, "I'm so glad, because it's the only language I speak." Although she looked like an immigrant, she was born and raised in the United States by highly acculturated parents.

SOCIAL FACTORS

Culture, however, needs to be distinguished from social influences on behavior, which, for our purposes, focus more on a social standing or condition such as educational level, income level, family structure, marital status, age, gender, sexual orientation, and employment or occupation. An argument can also be made to include race or ethnicity as a social factor because, like other social factors, being a member of an ethnic or racial category can predispose one to disadvantages or privileges, regardless of one's adherence to traditional or dominant cultural values or beliefs.

In summary, it is important to know the populations and subpopulations in the target area well before undertaking a needs assessment. As the vignette at the beginning of this chapter implies, examining the needs of subpopulations may reveal extreme needs among important subpopulations that would be hidden by averaging responses from the entire target area. Following are frequently overlooked social characteristics that may reveal differing patterns of needs for services. The list below serves as a reminder and checklist for designing an instrument:

_____ Ethnic group (e.g., Latinos or Mexican Americans, Polish Americans, Italian Americans, German Americans). Ethnicity should not be confused with race or racial categories or classifications, which typically are White or Caucasian, African American, Native American, and Asian American.

_____ Marital status

_____ Gender/sex

_____ Family structure (e.g., intact, single-parent, or blended families)

_____ Household income

_____ Educational attainment

_____ Employment status (employed/unemployed, full time/part time)

_____ Occupational status (including detailed or macro categories such as technical, unskilled laborer or blue-collar or white-collar workers)

_____ Housing status (defining this variable depends on need. Possible categories are renter/owner, living in public housing vs. nonpublic housing.)

_____ Health status (e.g., disabled, chronically ill, with mental health/emotional problems)

_____ Age

EXERCISES

An Asian immigrant resettlement program was recently funded by a major religious organization. Sandy was hired to run the program. She is a Caucasian woman who has no previous exposure to cultures other than her own. However, she is open minded and willing to learn. Approximately 100 Chinese families were sponsored by the religious organization and had arrived in the midwestern city four weeks ago. A needs assessment was planned about the housing, family, employment, dietary, and entertainment needs of these families.

Sandy plans to say the following sentence in Chinese to the immigrant families at tomorrow's program grand opening:

"I welcome you all to this the first day of your program!"

Sandy has had no help with translation, but she bought a Chinese-English dictionary that provides word-for-word translation and phonetic word information. Sandy began to translate word for word using the English word order.

1. What is the first step that Sandy should take before conducting a needs assessment?
2. What problems is she likely to encounter when she reads the translated sentence?
3. What type of translation should she follow?
4. When she translates questions for the needs assessment, what type of translation technique should she follow? Choose one and explain why: (a) one-way translation, (b) translation by committee, (c) double translation, (d) decentering.
5. What level of assimilation do you expect the Chinese families to be at—high, medium, or low? Why?
6. What are the three steps that Sandy needs to take to become culturally sensitive?

CONCLUSION

This book provided an introductory overview of various common needs assessments methods. It highlighted many important preliminary steps that need to be taken before choosing a particular methodology, including identifying key stakeholders in the outcomes of the assessment.

I emphasized the importance of developing a clear and concise purpose and key questions for needs assessments, which help to identify clearly the target populations and the scope of studies. Distinctions were emphasized between quantitative and qualitative methods and their implications for sample sizes, data preparation, coding, and analyses.

I also emphasized the importance of providing a logically organized report that presents the results of a needs assessment. Finally, I considered the importance of understanding the social and cultural context of respondents. Cultural and linguistic considerations were particularly emphasized and are offered as a special contribution of this book.

The appendix provides a listing of the literature on needs assessments and study methodology, useful for obtaining additional information on the subject. The appendix also contains a needs assessment guide to help the reader design and implement a needs assessment. This guide is simply a guide—it does not make decisions. However, the information in the main body of the book, along with the guide, will help the reader make the best decisions possible.

Needs assessments are important methods of gaining critical information needed by organizations to meet the human service needs of their target populations. Needs assessments are increasingly being required of organizations to continue their funding and justify their programs. This situation has sometimes led to negative or indifferent attitudes toward needs assessments by human service organizations being asked to conduct them.

In addition to attitudinal problems toward needs assessments, many assessments are hastily planned and poorly conceived, which leads to inferior data and unreliable results. Agencies and organizations need to see needs assessments as helpful ways of gaining vital information that can help ensure the success of their organizations. Doing so can increase their motivation to invest the necessary time in conducting one.

Regardless of interest by human service organizations, the diminishing amount of funding for community programs will undoubtedly lead to heightened competition for scarce funding as well as the need for greater justification for the services, products, or information rendered. Organizations would do well to conduct their own needs assessments before being mandated by external entities. As mentioned, needs assessments are adaptable to the amount of people and funding resources available. When possible, organizations should seek the assistance of researchers from universities and colleges, because they are often eager to assist. Suggestions were offered on ways to enlist the involvement of academic researchers.

This book is far from comprehensive. Many complex issues, such as statistical analysis, have been necessarily simplified for space reasons. However, the information included will help the reader gain a basic understanding of needs assessments and the steps needed to undertake one.

Needs assessments are being applied by various types of agencies, ranging from community-based organizations to large corporations. The literature on needs assessments can be found scattered in diverse fields such as the social sciences, business administration, education, and marketing. The reader is encouraged to build on the understanding of needs assessments gained here and to seek information from such sources as those represented among the references listed in the reference section.

APPENDIX
Needs Assessment Guide

INSTRUCTIONS

This guide is designed to help you think about the information needed to conduct a needs assessment. The guide does not focus on a particular subject or field. It can be used for designing needs assessments in most social service and human service fields. The guide is divided into the following eight sections:

    I. Purpose and Objectives
   II. Roles and Responsibilities
  III. Target Population and Subgroups
   IV. Stakeholders
    V. Resource Availability
   VI. Using the Information
  VII. Decision-Making Guide
VIII. General Checklist

Answer the questions in each section as completely as possible and follow additional instructions in the guide. Place a check mark next to the questions you cannot answer at this time. Seek out the information needed to answer any questions left blank before conducting a needs assessment.

At the end of the guide is a general checklist, which can help you identify the sections in which all questions have been answered. This guide is not all encompassing and should not be used alone. You will need to refer to other sources of information, such as the book and the reading material

in the reference section, before making final decisions about the design
and implementation of a needs assessment.

I. PURPOSE AND OBJECTIVES

    a. *General Purpose:* What is the purpose of conducting a needs assessment?

    b. *Objectives:* What are the key questions for which you need answers? The
    key questions determine the scope of a needs assessment and are directed
    at the purpose of the study.

    Caution: These questions will guide the data collected.

Key Questions:

1.

2.

3.

4.

5.

6.

7.

8.

9.

II. ROLES AND RESPONSIBILITIES

The following questions refer to those who are responsible for aspects of the needs assessment.

General Responsibility

a. Who is responsible for seeing that a needs assessment is conducted?

_____   _____
Name   Position
(More than one person, if appropriate.)

Specific Responsibilities

List individuals responsible for the following components of the needs assessment:

b. General Planning and Coordinating (all aspects of the study):

_____   _____
Name   Position
(More than one person, if appropriate.)

c. Designing the Study:

_____   _____
Name   Position
(More than one person, if appropriate.)

d. Collecting the Data:

_____   _____
Name   Position
(More than one person, if appropriate.)

e. Coding or Preparing the Data for Analysis:

_____   _____
Name   Position
(More than one person, if appropriate.)

f. Analyzing the Data (i.e., tabulating or noting the results without interpreting):

_____   _____
Name   Position
(More than one person, if appropriate.)

g. Interpreting the Results (i.e., give meaning to the data):

_____   _____
Name   Position
(More than one person, if appropriate.)

h. Reporting the Results:

_____   _____
Name   Position
(More than one person, if appropriate.)

Stop and consider those people delegated responsibilities. Ask yourself these questions:

                                                                    YES/NO

Are they being granted release time to
accomplish these responsibilities?   _____

Do they have the needed interest and skills
or are they able or willing to acquire them
to accomplish their assigned task(s)?   _____

If a group effort, are members of this group
willing and able to work together, have the
opportunity to do so, and communicate with
one another enough to accomplish the entire
task?   _____

If any responses to these questions are no, reassign personnel and responsibilities or consider contracting the needs assessment or parts of it to outside experts (e.g., university researchers, private research contractors, parent agency, consultants, and so on).

Overseeing Committee

Form an overseeing committee, made up of internal and external members of the organization. At least one member of the target community should be a part of this committee. Ethnic minority members should also be included, if reflective of the target population.

i. Describe the membership of the overseeing committee.
    Number of members: _____
    Number of members from the target population: _____
    Number of members who are ethnic minorities
    reflective of target population: _____

j. Indicate how often the committee will meet.

Will the overseeing committee be used to oversee:

k. Ethics?
_____ Yes _____ No _____ Not sure (Please determine.)

If no, explain who will:

l. Wording of Questionnaire?
_____ Yes _____ No _____ Not sure (Please determine.)

If no, explain who will:

m. Cultural Sensitivity and Relevance?
_____ Yes _____ No _____ Not sure (Please determine.)

If no, explain who will:

n. General Appropriateness of Study Design and Plans to Implement It?
_____ Yes _____ No _____ Not sure (Please determine.)

If no, explain who will:

III. TARGET POPULATION AND SUBGROUPS

These questions pertain to the targeted population for the needs assessment and the relevant subgroups.

a. What are the physical boundaries delineating the target area?

b. Describe the target population. Use demographic or other key characteristics important for defining who is and is not a member of the target population.

c. Is it important for you specifically to compare needs among ethnic groups?
   ___ Yes ___ No

d. If yes, check off the ethnic groups you need information from:
   ___ Anglo Americans
   ___ Hispanics/Latinos
   ___ African Americans
   ___ Native Americans
   ___ Asians
   ___ Others: _____
   _____

e. For each subgroup marked, indicate how you will determine ethnic group membership (self-identification?).

f. Is it important for you specifically to compare needs between gender groups?
   ___ Yes ___ No

g. If yes, will you want 50% of each in your sample?
   ___ Yes ___ No

h. Is it important for you to compare subgroups differing in education (e.g., high school vs. college graduates)?
   ___ Yes ___ No

i. If yes, describe the different education subgroups and how you will define each:

j. Is it important for you to compare subgroups differing in income levels (e.g., family income under $10,000 vs. more than this amount)?
   ___ Yes ___ No

k. If yes, define each subgroup:

l. Are there other specialized subgroups in your target population about which you need specific data?
   ___ Yes ___ No

m. If yes, list and describe each specialized subgroup (e.g., elderly, adolescents, females, drug users, gang members, violent offenders):

IV. STAKEHOLDERS

List all who have some responsibility for commissioning a needs assessment, whether internal or external to your organization. Place them in order of decision-making influence from the most influential* in commissioning and directing the implementation of a needs assessment to the least influential (list names and affiliation to the organization needing the assessment).

Circle the number for those who must be satisfied in the undertaking of a needs assessment. Indicate the general type of assessment they expect (quantitative or qualitative) and list the reason for their preference. Determine the number of appropriate persons.

Name   Affiliation to Your Organization

(1) _____   _____

Type of Needs Assessment Desired or Expected by This Person:

_____ Quantitative

_____ Qualitative

_____ Doesn't care

_____ Not sure (Please find out)

Indicate reason for choice and list other requirements: _____

_____

_____

Name   Affiliation to Your Organization

(2) _____   _____

Type of Needs Assessment Desired or Expected by This Person:

_____ Quantitative

_____ Qualitative

_____ Doesn't care

_____ Not sure (Please find out)

Indicate reason for choice and list other requirements: _____

_____

_____

*"Influential persons" are those who need to be satisfied, and for whom there are positive or negative consequences (e.g., redo/acclaim the needs assessment, praise/criticize the implementing organization, increase/maintain/withdraw agency's funds).

Name   Affiliation to Your Organization

(3) _____   _____

Type of Needs Assessment Desired or Expected by This Person:

_____ Quantitative

_____ Qualitative

_____ Doesn't care

_____ Not sure (Please find out)

Indicate reason for choice and list other requirements: _____

_____

_____

Name   Affiliation to Your Organization

(4) _____   _____

Type of Needs Assessment Desired or Expected by This Person:

_____ Quantitative

_____ Qualitative

_____ Doesn't care

_____ Not sure (Please find out)

Indicate reason for choice and list other requirements: _____

_____

_____

Name   Affiliation to Your Organization

(5) _____   _____

Type of Needs Assessment Desired or Expected by This Person:

_____ Quantitative

_____ Qualitative

_____ Doesn't care

_____ Not sure (Please find out)

Indicate reason for choice and list other requirements: _____

_____

_____

Name   Affiliation to Your Organization

(6) _____   _____

Type of Needs Assessment Desired or Expected by This Person:

_____ Quantitative

_____ Qualitative

_____ Doesn't care

_____ Not sure (Please find out)

Indicate reason for choice and list other requirements: _____

_____

_____

Name   Affiliation to Your Organization

(7) _____   _____

Type of Needs Assessment Desired or Expected by This Person:

_____ Quantitative

_____ Qualitative

_____ Doesn't care

_____ Not sure (Please find out)

Indicate reason for choice and list other requirements: _____

_____

_____

V. RESOURCE AVAILABILITY

a. List the amount of funds you have to conduct a needs assessment: $ _____

b. List the people who will help conduct the needs assessment and indicate if they have training or experience in conducting needs assessments.

Name	Title	Research Training? (Circle)
1. _____	_____	Yes - No
2. _____	_____	Yes - No
3. _____	_____	Yes - No
4. _____	_____	Yes - No
5. _____	_____	Yes - No
6. _____	_____	Yes - No
7. _____	_____	Yes - No

c. List any language capability they possess that can be used to interact with study participants who may not have a command of English:

Languages:_____

_____

_____

d. List cultural training or experience these same persons hold that may be used for collecting data for the needs assessment.

Cultural Training/Experience: _____

_____

_____

e. Check off the equipment and supplies you have access to. Check all that apply:

_____ Printing equipment (e.g., photocopy machine)

_____ Computer with statistical analysis program

_____ Computer with wordprocessing software

_____ Postage

_____ Transportation—vehicle or reimbursal for car

_____ Work space and storage space for study materials

_____ Other equipment or supplies:_____

_____

f. How much time do you have to undertake a needs assessment from start to finish?

Time in months: _____

g. Is this amount inflexible?

_____ Yes _____ No _____ Not sure (Please find out.)

VI. USING THE INFORMATION

a. Indicate the expected uses of the results of the study. Check off all that apply.

Results from the needs assessment will enable you to:

_____ Alter organization functions and services as appropriate

_____ Fulfill a requirement by your sponsors

_____ Fulfill another externally imposed requirement (which?): _____

_____

_____ Be used to support existing views and perceptions

_____ Justify existence of organization

_____ Use information to generate additional funding

_____ Other: _____

_____

_____

b. Are two needs assessments being planned for a pre/post evaluation study?
   _____ Yes _____ No

c. How do you plan to report the results of the needs assessment? Select one:

_____ A written comprehensive report

_____ A formal, but short, written report

_____ A short and informally written report

_____ Only a verbal presentation

_____ Other: _____

_____

d. Who will be responsible for documenting the results of the study?
   Person(s): _____

_____

VII. DECISION-MAKING GUIDE

Place a check mark next to the most appropriate response to each question below. Use your previous responses in the guide to help you respond to the questions.

a. Type of needs assessment:

_____ Quantitative

_____ Qualitative

_____ Mixed

_____ Other: _____

_____ Not sure. Explain: _____

_____

b. Type of questionnaire or data source:

_____ Secondary data

_____ Interview

_____ Key informant

_____ Focus group

_____ Survey

_____ Other:_____

_____ Not sure. Explain: _____

_____

c. Form of questions to ask:

_____ Open ended

_____ Structured (fixed choice)

_____ Semistructured

_____ Other:_____

_____ Not sure. Explain: _____

_____

d. Will your sample be stratified (i.e., participants selected based on such demographic characteristics as gender, ethnicity, income, education)?

_____ Yes _____ No _____ Not sure

Explain:_____

_____

e. If yes, what are your stratifying variables?

_____ Gender/sex

_____ Ethnicity

_____ Income

_____ Education

_____ Age

_____ Other: _____

_____ Other: _____

_____ Other: _____

f. How many participants do feel you need?

Number: _____

g. If selecting a stratified sample, how many participants will you need in each stratum (e.g., gender: 30 men and 30 women)?

Stratum (Variable)	Number in Each Strata Needed
_____	_____ _____ _____ _____
_____	_____ _____ _____ _____
_____	_____ _____ _____ _____
_____	_____ _____ _____ _____

h. Participant Selection Method to Be Used:

_____ Based on participant's expertise (focus/key informant)

_____ Quota sampling method

_____ Interval

_____ Judgment

_____ Systematic

_____ Snowball

_____ Other: _____

_____ Not sure. Explain: _____

_____

_____

i. What types of demographic variables will you include in your question-naire (e.g., gender, ethnicity)?

_____ _____ _____

_____ _____ _____

_____ _____ _____

_____ _____ _____

_____ _____ _____

If none, state why:_____

_____

_____

j. Will you conduct a pretest?

_____ Yes _____ No _____ Not sure

If no or not sure, explain why: _____

_____

_____

If yes, how many participants will you need?

Number: _____

k. Select the type of statistical analysis you will use:

_____ Descriptive

_____ Inferential

_____ Mixed

_____ Other:_____

VIII. GENERAL CHECKLIST

Place a check mark next to each section title below that you have addressed satisfactorily. Indicate other concerns that need to be satisfied before conducting a needs assessment.

_____   I. Purpose and Objectives

_____   II. Roles and Responsibilities

_____ III. Targeted Population and Subgroups

_____ IV. Stakeholders

_____   V. Resource Availability

_____ VI. Use of the Information

_____ Other (Please indicate):

_____ Other (Please indicate):

_____ Other (Please indicate):

REFERENCES

Baker, B. O., Hardyck, C. D., & Petrinovich, L. F. (1966). Weak measurements vs. strong statistics: An empirical critique of S. S. Stevens' proscriptions on statistics. *Educational and Psychological Measurement, 26,* 291-309.

Berger, R. M., & Patchner, M. A. (1988a). *Planning for research: A guide for the helping professions.* Newbury Park, CA: Sage.

Berger, R. M., & Patchner, M. A. (1988b). *Implementing the research plan: A guide for the helping professions.* Newbury Park, CA: Sage.

Blythe, B. J., & Tripodi, T. (1989). *Measurement in direct practice.* Newbury Park, CA: Sage.

Cohen, J. (1988). *Statistical power analysis for the behavioral sciences* (2nd ed.). Hillsdale, NJ: Lawrence Erlbaum.

Coley, S. M., & Scheinberg, C. A. (1990). *Proposal writing.* Newbury Park, CA: Sage.

Cook, T. D., & Levitan, L. C. (1985). Program evaluation. In G. Lindzey & E. Aronson (Eds.), *Handbook of social psychology* (Vol. 2, pp. 699-777). New York: Random House.

de Vaus, D. A. (1990). *Surveys in social research* (2nd ed.). Boston, MA: Allen & Unwin.

Debus, M., & Porter, N. (1989). *Methodological review: A handbook for excellence in focus group research.* Washington, DC: Academy for Educational Development Healthcom.

Gibson, G. (1983). *Our kingdom stands on brittle glass.* Silver Spring, MD: National Association of Social Workers.

Gilbert, T. (1967, Fall). Praxeonomy: A systematic approach to identifying training needs. *Management of Personnel Quarterly,* p. 20.

Glass, G. V., & Stanley, J. C. (1970). *Statistical methods in education and psychology.* Englewood Cliffs, NJ: Prentice Hall.

Goldstein, I. L. (1986). *Training in organizations: Needs assessment, development, and evaluation* (2nd ed.). Monterey, CA: Brooks/Cole.

Harrison, A. O., Wilson, M. N., Pine, C. J., Chan, S. Q., & Buriel, R. (1991). Family ecologies of ethnic minority children. *Child Development, 61,* 347-362.

Holt, K., Geschka, H., & Peterlongo, G. (1984). *Need assessment: A key to user-oriented product innovation.* New York: John Wiley.

Johnson, D. E., Meiller, L. R., Miller, L. C., & Summers, G. F. (1987). *Needs assessment: Theory and methods.* Ames: Iowa State University Press.

Kalton, G. (1983). *Introduction to survey sampling.* Beverly Hills, CA: Sage.

Kaufman, R., & English, F. (1979). *Needs assessment: Concept and application.* Englewood Cliffs, NJ: Educational Technology.

Keefe, S., & Padilla, A. M. (1987). *Chicano ethnicity.* Albuquerque: University of New Mexico Press.

Kettner, P. M., Moroney, R. M., & Martin, L. L. (1990). *Designing and managing programs: An effectiveness-based approach.* Newbury Park, CA: Sage.

Larson, M. L. (1984). *Meaning-based translation: A guide to cross-language equivalence.* New York: University Press of America.

Lauffer, A. (1982). *Assessment tools: For practitioners, managers, and trainers.* Beverly Hills, CA: Sage.

Levy, C. V. (1972). *A primer for community research.* San Francisco, CA: Far West Research.

Marcus, H. R., & Kitayama, S. (1991). Culture and the self: Implications for cognition, emotion, and motivation. *Psychological Review, 98*(2), 224-253.

Marin, G., & Marin, B. V. (1991). *Research with Hispanic populations.* Newbury Park, CA: Sage.

Moore, J. W. (1991). *Going down to the barrio: Homeboys and homegirls in change.* Philadelphia, PA: Temple University Press.

Neuber, K. A., with Atkins, W. T., Jacobson, J. A., & Reuteman, N. A. (1980). *Needs assessment: A model for community planning.* Beverly Hills, CA: Sage.

Nickens, J. M., Purga, A. J., & Noriega, P. P. (1980). *Research methods for needs assessment.* Washington, DC: University Press of America.

Pietrzak, J., Ramler, M., Renner, T., Ford., L. & Gilbert, N. (1990). *Practical program evaluation: Examples from child abuse prevention.* Newbury Park, CA: Sage.

Ramirez, M., & Castaneda, A. (1974). *Cultural democracy, bicognitive development and education.* New York: Academic Press.

Rutman, L., & Mowbray, G. (1983). *Understanding program evaluation.* Beverly Hills, CA: Sage.

Schaefer, M. (1987). *Implementing change in service programs: Project planning and management.* Newbury Park, CA: Sage.

Soriano, F. I. (1993). Cultural sensitivity and gang intervention. In A. P. Goldstein & C. R. Huff (Eds.), *The gang intervention handbook* (pp. 441-463). Champaign, IL: Research Press.

Ulschak, F. L. (1983). *Human resource development: The theory and practice of needs assessment.* Reston, VA: Reston.

Zautra, A., Bachrach, K., & Hess, R. (1983). *Strategies for needs assessment in prevention.* New York: Haworth Press.

ABOUT THE AUTHOR

Fernando I. Soriano is Assistant Professor in the Department of Behavioral Science at the University of Missouri in Kansas City. He recently returned to Missouri after spending two years as Visiting Professor of Psychology and Education at Stanford University. He is an applied researcher and academician who has written numerous publications focusing on such social problems as gang membership, youth violence, delinquency, substance abuse, AIDS, and the health and oral health care status of minorities. He sits on several national committees, including the Commission on Violence and Youth for the American Psychological Association and the National Advisory Committee for the Gang Drug Abuse Prevention Program sponsored by the Administration for Children, Youth, and Families. He has been involved in community program development and evaluation for several years.